AI Unleashed: Sparking Innovation and Curiosity in Young Minds

Dr. Selva Sugunendran

CEng, MIEE, MCMI, CHt, MIMDHA, MBBNLP, MGONLP, DBS
AI Robotics Strategist & Visionary Author
#1 Best Selling Author, Speaker & Coach
Website: https://AIRoboticsForGood.com
Email: Selva@AIRoboticsForGood.com

Copyright © 2024 by DR. Selva

"AI Unleashed: Sparking Innovation and Curiosity in Young Minds"

All rights reserved. No part of this book may be reproduced or transmitted in any form or by any means, electronic or mechanical, including photocopying, recording, or by any information storage retrieval system, without permission in writing from the Copyright owner.

Medical Disclaimer: The author of this book is a competent,

experienced writer. He has taken every opportunity to ensure that all information presented here is correct and up to date at the time of writing. No documentation within this book has been evaluated by the Food and Drug Administration, and no documentation should be used to diagnose, treat, cure, or prevent any disease.

Any information is to be used for educational and information purposes only. It should never be substituted for the medical advice from your doctor or other health care professionals.

We do not dispense medical advice, prescribe drugs, or diagnose any illnesses with our literature.

The author and publisher are not responsible or liable for any self or third-party diagnosis made by visitors based upon the content of this book. The author or publisher does not in any way endorse any commercial products or services linked from other websites to this book.

Please, always consult your doctor or health care specialist if you are in any way concerned about your physical wellbeing.

BOOK TITLES

Each title attempts to distil the book's manifesto – helping young people take over AI, indeed take over the future.

Hello & Welcome!

If you have been looking at the title of the book, let me say, any of the following titles would apply to the contents of this book:

1. "Empowering Tomorrow: A Guide to Inspiring AI Leaders in the Next Generation"

2. "AI Unleashed: Sparking Innovation and Curiosity in Young Minds"

3. "The Future Begins Now: Cultivating AI Talent in Youth"

4. "Nurturing the Innovators of Tomorrow: A Journey Through AI Education"

5. "Rising with AI: Empowering the Next Generation of Digital Pioneers"

6. "From Curiosity to Creation: Guiding Young Learners in the World of AI"

7. "The Path to Tomorrow: Inspiring Young Minds with AI and Innovation"

All these titles emphasise the radical newness of the technologies associated with AI, the prime focus looking to optimise the learning practices of the young, and the allure of perfection and optimal performance – all of which might seem attractive to the young who are keen to improve their skills and performance.

"AI Unleashed: Sparking Innovation and Curiosity in Young Minds"

ABOUT THE BOOK

The world is changing faster than most of us could have imagined, and much of that change is driven by Artificial Intelligence (AI). As an AI Robotics Strategist and a Visionary Author, and someone who cares about the future of technology and its users, I have had a ringside seat on the potential of AI to transform and infuse many domains, improve the lives of many globally, and help face some of the big macro challenges of the near future. But with potential comes responsibility: a commitment to ensure that the next generation hears the same clarion call to prepare for, and harness the potentials of, work and life in an AI world.

It is in this spirit, then, that I am pleased to present this book, which brings together 21 thought-provoking articles about the crucially important role of AI as an educational resource for learners of all ages and, especially, for youngsters who will be the leaders of the fourth industrial revolution. Moreover, the articles spell out how it is possible to bring these learners along, to engage and equip the young, to inspire and educate the 1.8 billion boys and girls who today are under the age of 15. If you are a parent, a teacher, a mentor, or anyone else concerned with the future, with the way ahead, with what young people will need to engender and build this future through effective collaboration together with their peers, these articles will speak directly to you and provide pathways of transition and strategy, visions and artifacts, stories, and case studies, and, above all, a real sense of how we can motivate kids to learn AI.

It's hard to overstate the need for AI literacy: as we roll further into the 21st century, AI will be at the heart of almost every sector of the economy – from healthcare and finance to entertainment and education. The jobs of the near future will depend on skills that don't yet exist. It will depend on workers with the ability to not only use but to shape AI. But technical skills alone will be insufficient. We also need to foster creativity, ethical consciousness, and a passion for lifelong learning – qualities that will help young people not only adapt to change, but also to shape it.

Here, we've collected some of our best stories addressing a wide range of topics, such as how to make AI learning fun and engaging, how to remove obstacles and make AI available to everyone, and how to foster the talents of young innovators. In these articles you'll generally find a good overview of the opportunities and difficulties of AI education, and sensible advice to anyone interested in supporting the next generation.

Because that is the spirit in which I, a career explorer of the frontiers of AI and robotics, approach my research. I'm empowered by my imagination, my curiosity, to put one foot in front of another – and that power is what robots need if they ever become truly autonomous, truly creative. It's that same drive that has carried humans to dominate our planet and connect a world with billions of interesting brains. That's why I am so very keen for all young people to get their hands on AI. Experiencing the inside of a robot is not just learning about technology. It's learning to imagine, to create, to lead.

With this book, we call upon every young person to believe in herself or himself as a creator, an innovator, and a leader in the age of AI; and for all of us to take a stand to invest in generations to come.

I invite you to take this journey with an open mind, and a determination to make a difference, and help to build a world in which technology augments, rather than replaces, humanity.

Thank you for extending your undertaking. Let us inspire and help those who will be the future torchbearers for innovation.

Dr. Selva

ABOUT THE AUTHOR

DR SELVA SUGUNENDRAN has performed many lofty positions in life, The most uplifting to him is the one he chose, which was to serve mankind by showing them the way to health, wealth, and success.

Upon selling his UK based Integrated High Security IT company which he ran for 25 years as the company owner, he took the "jump" out of the corporate world into his passion for helping people to be more, do more and get more out of their life than they ever thought possible! Young or old, he helped them create a new blueprint for life that literally changed their world and continues to do so.

As a result of that work, he was attracted to study, research, write and publish 50+ books of which 6 books were #1 Best Sellers in genres Health & Wellness,

Alzheimer's / Dementia, Success in Business &Life, and Christianity & more recently on AI & Robotics

He has developed a special Ai- Robotic Machine (which is currently in a prototype stage) which can be used as a "Virtual Carer" for Dementia patients who live alone and cannot afford 24-hour care.

His books on Ai were prepared for people who are NOT experts on AI, so that they can learn about AI and Robotics, the power of AI as well as pros and cons including ethical considerations.

The current book is the tenth in the series of books on AI Robotics. The prime focus of this book is looking to optimise the learning practices of the young, and the allure of perfection and optimal performance – all of which might seem attractive to the young who are keen to improve their skills and performance.

TABLE OF CONTENTS

Here are 21 article titles focused on motivating young people to learn AI. Each of these headlines is meant to grab attention, emphasise the need for education around AI, and offer actionable suggestions for engaging younger learners, respectively.

Here you go!

ABOUT THE BOOK v
ABOUT THE AUTHOR ix
TABLE OF CONTENTS xi
INTRODUCTION xiv

CHAPTER 1: The Future is Now: Why Young Minds Should Embrace AI 1

CHAPTER 2: Unlocking Potential: How AI Learning Can Empower the Next Generation 6

CHAPTER 3: 10 Ways to Make AI Fun and Engaging for Young Learners 13

CHAPTER 4: Inspiring Tomorrow's Innovators: The Role of AI in Youth Education 20

CHAPTER 5: From Gamers to Coders: Transforming Passion into AI Skills 26

CHAPTER 6: AI for All: Breaking Down Barriers for Young Learners 34

CHAPTER 7: The Digital Playground: How to Make AI Learning Exciting for Kids.. 42

CHAPTER 8: Why Every Young Person Should Learn AI: A Parent's Guide 50

CHAPTER 9: AI and the Youth: Building the Innovators of the Future 58

CHAPTER 10: Nurturing Curiosity: How AI Can Spark a Lifelong Love of Learning 67

CHAPTER 11: Coding is Cool: How to Get Young People Excited About AI 74

CHAPTER 12: AI Adventures: Fun Projects to Get Kids Hooked on Technology 82

CHAPTER 13: The power of AI: how to inspire the next generation of tech leaders 92

CHAPTER 14: Demystifying AI: A Beginner's Guide for Young Enthusiasts 100

CHAPTER 15: From Curiosity to Career: The Benefits of Learning AI Early" 108

CHAPTER 16: Engaging the Digital Natives: Innovative Ways to Teach AI 116

CHAPTER 17: AI Literacy: Preparing Young Minds for the Jobs of Tomorrow 125

CHAPTER 18: The Joy of Discovery: Encouraging Young Learners to Explore AI 134

CHAPTER 19: Youth and AI: Cultivating Skills for a Tech-Driven World 145

CHAPTER 20: Turning Imagination into Innovation: How AI Can Inspire Young Creators 154

CHAPTER 21: Learning AI Through Play: How to Make Technology Fun for Kids 163

CONCLUSION 172

PART II: SELECTED BOOKS BY THE AUTHOR 175

APPENDICES 185

INTRODUCTION

Empowering the Next Generation

The Importance of AI-Education for Youth

While many typewritten stories about artificial intelligence (AI) could be something out of The Terminator or "I, Robot", in today's digital atmosphere, AI is no longer something out of fiction. The use of computers to create machines with the ability to mimic human-like thought is in industry, the economy, and the workplace right now. Smartphones sit at our fingertips, more and more websites offer algorithm-based recommendations to what we should watch and read, and innovation is happening at a speed of light. As simple as it seems, if you've ever used a GPS system to figure out directions before, you have already experienced AI.

Understanding it is not a luxury for your average 12-year-old, but a vital necessity of life The future everyday life for the 'digital natives' — children born from 1995 to 2010, and the adolescents that have come of age after them — is, predictably and rightly, high-tech. They are 'digital natives': they know how to use the technology, but how to build and guide it? For this, they must learn about AI.

This book is about inspiring the inspiration. It's about parents and educators and other mentors who are trying to figure out how to teach kids about AI. So, the individual pieces in this book are about everything from 'how can we make learning about AI fun and cool?' to 'what do we need to do to inculcate ethical awareness within young people who are engaged with AI?' to 'how can we help prepare kids for jobs of the future associated with AI?' So, you have a whole array of important topics in here about what we need to do to enlist the next generation for the AI onrush of our lives and our work — and in every instance, hopefully, people will not only get a sense of motivation about this critical subject, but we'll give them some practical ideas of things they can do.

They should understand that learning AI isn't just a means to a more practical end but is an end in itself – preparation for a creative and exhilarating life as innovator, leader and changemaker. And, if young people are all those things, imagine the kind of impact they can make on humanity and the planet as collaborators with their AI tools, addressing the challenges of a dangerous and rapidly changing world, creating new technologies to repair it and moving it in a humane and sustainable direction. To realise this potential, our young people need help. We need to set them on the right path, provide the right resources, and give them the encouragement they need.

This book is a call to arms. It's about realising the potential of young minds, by providing them with the keys to unlock it; about turning curiosity into knowledge, and knowledge into power. Whether you're a parent of a young person with an interest in AI, a teacher eager to inspire your pupils or a mentor wanting to nurture the next generation of tech leaders, this book provides the basics you'll need to help them launch their AI careers.

With our combined efforts, we can foster the schoolkids of tomorrow, and prepare them for a future with AI as an integral part of it. The articles collected in this book are merely a start – a means to have a look, to make, to show and to explore the wonders of Artificial Intelligence.

Welcome to the journey of empowering the next generation through AI education.

Let's get started!

CHAPTER 1

The Future is Now: Why Young Minds Should Embrace AI

Going into the 21st century, the weaving of artificial intelligence (AI) into human life is happening with ever-accelerating speed. From Siri and Alexa to the complex algorithms driving our driverless cars, AI is on its way to being part of virtually every aspect of the way we live, work, and interact with our environment. For the young adults of today, being able to grasp and use AI is no longer nice to have, but a must.

The Growing Importance of AI

The dream of a world run like the machines of science fiction has ceased being science fiction. AI is unfolding right now in the real world, at an unprecedented pace that is quickly transforming industries, economies, and societies. In 2025, a report by the World Economic Forum predicts, there will be 58 million new jobs created by AI. And they will demand entirely new skills that aren't taught in most schools and universities. They will demand, especially, machine learning and AI.

With a high demand for such knowledge in the (job) market of the future, there is no question that these technologies become a subject focused on at an early age. As we live in a technological age, a command of AI will thrive in students that begin work on it from an early age; it will give them an early advantage compared to those that do not.

AI as a Tool for Innovation

Beyond its career opportunities, AI also stands for the change of innovation and creation. Youngsters have always been the engines of growth, and innovation will continue to thrive through their unique voices. By learning AI, they can utilise this power to come up with solutions for the problems we face, from public healthcare to education, climate change and inequality.

Furthermore, the democratising impacts of AI could extend to fostering innovation among younger generations. Innovation requires experimenting with lots of ideas, which indicates the need for looser and more open environments in which to play and learn. Livestock farmers refer to cows as 'liquid gold' because they procure manure from livestock that can be collected and aged in a manure pit before being spread evenly across pastures, creating more usable land for cattle-rearing. In this regard, Google's widely prominent AIY Projects and IBM's more affordable Watson technologies can provide students of all backgrounds and levels of technical knowhow with access to AI, thus enabling them to develop various projects through experimentation and prototyping.

Overcoming the Challenges

While there's no debate about the manifold benefits, the challenge with motivating youth to learn AI lies less in the subject itself than in our own approaches to teaching it. The first hurdle is perception. When we teach AI, there's a strong tendency to frame it as something that's 'complex' or 'difficult', when the core concepts are rather elementary and very approachable.

Interactive learning tools and hands-on projects could be also a great approach to make AI more relatable: plenty of platforms that introduce children to programming, such as Scratch and Python, develop users' designing and art skills through small projects that help grow their knowledge of AI in an enjoyable and creative way. An alternative could also be the use of storytelling, if pictured in an effective way, to show how AI's functioning can be applied to the daily life of young students.

The Role of Educators and Parents

Educators and parents can do much to encourage young people to find AI accessible and interesting by emphasising a growth mindset and curiosity, because these things are so relevant to AI learning. Creating an education approach to AI would not only help people learn an important technological subject, but also inspire in young people a sense that this is an exciting area of learning full of opportunities rather than an enemy to be feared.

We all need to integrate AI into our scholarly lives, but what's just as crucial is creating spaces that permit us to play with the technology and feel safe experimenting with it so we can make mistakes as we learn. Learning AI is a process, and like any creative or technical endeavour, it takes patience, practice, and tenacity.

Parents might also provide their children with resources and children-friendly opportunities to dive into AI: coding camps and competitions, for instance, or time to work on defining their own AI projects at home.

Conclusion: Embracing the Future

The future is here, powered by AI. Learning AI is essential for today's younger generation, beyond staying competitive in the open labour market and earning a living. The world of tomorrow needs creative learners who have mastered the art of AI and become builders and craftsmen of our shared future.

We can help empower the next generation to face these challenges by making AI accessible to young people and encouraging them to not only use it, but also understand it, enjoy it, and, we hope, one day create it.

DR. SELVA SUGUNENDRAN

CHAPTER 2

Unlocking Potential: How AI Learning Can Empower the Next Generation

The relentless pace of innovation in artificial intelligence (AI) has the potential to revolutionise many industries and sectors. Developing proficiency in AI today might well become the major opportunity for the young to harness their innate skills, all to transform the global human system for the better.

The Transformative Power of AI

For learners of any age, AI will govern almost everything they experience and thus it becomes imperative that they learn about AI. It's not enough to know how to use ridesharing apps or social media. Young learners must learn about AI, not just because the tech-driven global economy requires it, but also so that they can engage as informed citizens.

Learning AI can empower the next generation in several keyways:

1. Critical thinking and problem-solving improvement: For instance, AI education not only embraces the idea of teaching children to think critically through complex problems but also stresses the importance of problem-solving in this area. Students working on AI projects can learn not only to break down complex tasks into smaller manageable problems but also to conduct data analysis and find solutions based on key algorithms. Unlike learning how to solve traditional math problems, these skills are not only useful for AI but also for academic and practical life, because they can be applied to many other areas.

2. Developing creativity and innovation: AI technology brings endless opportunities. Whether it's creating a next-generation app, a game or a real-life situation, AI gives each student the resources to create and invent the solutions to real issues. Embracing the use of AI allows the younger generation to bring real-life solutions to the global community, and further develop the world's technology innovations.

3. Developing Confidence and Resilience: Learning AI is unquestionably difficult. And yet doing hard things feels good to us as humans. When we push through a challenging task and achieve success, we feel a sense of competence. That sense of empowerment spurs us to push even further, to take on the next challenge – and the next after that.

4. Skilling Up for the Future Job Market: Skills in AI are in high demand and will likely be in higher demand going forward. Learning AI can set you up for success in the job market of the future, where AI and related technologies will be dominant. This could be a job in AI, but it could also just be using some of your skills in another, unrelated field – regardless of your chosen profession, having strong AI skills will set you up for success.

Making AI Accessible to All

An important challenge in the education of AI is how to ensure that every student can participate, growing their curiosity and understanding of AI – regardless of their background or activity and interest level. To nurture the potential of future generations on a broad scale, inclusive learning environments are needed that suit diverse learning styles and needs.

Here are some strategies to make AI education more accessible:

1. Engaging Interactive Tools: Playing with interactive tools and platforms can make learning AI more fun and accessible. Newer coding platforms such as Scratch and Code.org feature some AI-related projects designed for beginners, to help them learn AI in a culturally relevant way. These interactive tools are designed to be simple to use, so students can try making things without needing to know how to code («scratching the surface» of the source code).

2. Embed Embodied Experiences: Hands-on embodied experiences can make AI concrete and help students make connections between the ideas and real-world examples of AI. Students can elect to pursue one or more hands-on projects such as creating a simple chatbot, a recommendation system, or a machine learning model, for example.

3. Organise Participation Resources and Support: Available resources and support vary from student ensure that the education offered by AI can be reaped by all students, it is important to provide resources such as tutorials, online courses and mentoring to those in need. Schools, communities and organisations will play the key role in providing these resources and help students to learn AI.

4. Encouraging Diversity and Inclusion: Diversity and inclusion are crucial in AI education, and by encouraging as many participants as possible across the widest possible spectrum, and by exposing students (and citizen groups) to diverse perspectives in AI, we can better foster true AI leaders of tomorrow's generation who reflect our current, diverse society. This is important not only for equity but for the innovation and creativity viewed as crucial for progress in AI.

The Role of Educators and Parents:

Teachers and parents have the power to enable learners to maximise their potential in AI. A growth mindset, curiosity, and the freedom to explore will serve students well in an AI-filled world.

Educators can give AI a role in the curriculum (for instance by introducing AI concepts in math, science and computer science classes) and outside the curriculum (by providing opportunities for afterschool programming classes, coding clubs, and AI competitions, such as 'hackathons').

Of course, parents need to provide some support for their kids' interest in AI — such as material, a place to tinker, access to books, public libraries, YouTube here and there, encouragement in independent projects, and access to mentorship or role models in the field in the machine-learning domain and on platforms such as Kickstarter etc. Overall, a supportive home is the best environment to seed a love of learning and a passion for AI.

Conclusion: Empowering the Next Generation

With learning AI, the next generation can unlock their potential, acquire these 21st-century and in fact lifelong skills imperative in preparation for a future unimaginable yet to come. AI is not just a technology; it is the technology of empowerment.

Our job, as teachers, parents, and mentors, is to make this kind of AI education accessible – to train and equip future generations to master, dominate and ultimately transform AI into a force of humanity, as they become the true successors and (hopefully) changemakers of our AI future.

CHAPTER 3

10 Ways to Make AI Fun and Engaging for Young Learners

"Artificial intelligence' is not a particularly sexy phrase when splashed across a school wall. In truth, 'artificial intelligence' is a bit too cool for school – so, how does anyone get younger learners excited about minds that might equal or exceed human intelligence? If the spirit of the future is to be infused into the school room (as I believe it must), how can you convince a student: 'You should really be learning this.'? Here are 10 suggestions. 1. Make it fun You're 13, so it doesn't really matter; what you want to do is learn how to ...

1. Start with Games and Interactive Projects

Gamification – using games to teach – can be a great way to help young learners begin to grasp the concepts behind AI. There are plenty of AI-assisted games and playful projects that can be used to make learning about AI an exciting experience. For instance, Code Combat and the open-ended AI story generator AI Dungeon offer gamified teaching of coding and AI, respectively in a playful environment.

They first learn about AI concepts via playing, so they don't feel like they're doing 'schoolwork'.

2. Relate AI to Real-Life Examples

One thing we can do is give kids connections to AI through things that are tangible in their world as they grow up and go to school. How does AI power some of your favourite apps, video games and social media platforms? How are the recommendations you get online generated? How does AI enable new applications such as self-driving cars, virtual assistants for the home and search engines?

3. Encourage Creative AI Projects

Coding and algorithms are only a small part of an AI system; the other persistently shadowy element is the huge amounts of data that it digests. It is precisely this imbued data, mined from the world, that constitutes the real inventive power of AI. So, as well as teaching technical skills such as code writing, ask students to learn how to apply AI technologies in creative projects: ask them to develop a video game, create digital art or music. For example, Google's Deep Dream and the OpenAI music engine Muse Net are easy ways to get students thinking creatively about AI. Using AI can be a real joy, and it will reward the effort.

4. Use Storytelling to Explain AI Concepts

And regardless of how you approach explaining your research, there's at least one method you should always use: you should frame your explanation as a story. Humans love stories, and stories are a perfect vehicle for delivering a complex idea. If you can make an analogy between the core idea you're trying to get across and some element of a story, you could go a long way toward helping people to understand virtual entities, massive unfalsifiable hypotheses and nonlinear dynamic processes that adaptively filter and provide feedback to systems – all of which are key to understanding your research. Human intuition kicks in when you hit someone in the face with the idea that AI is a symbol, input, concept, metaphor, perpetually convening committee, black box or virtual entity. If you're feeling adventurous about using a story to convey your thesis, try to let us see the main ideas physically interacting with other ideas as they encounter problems, solve puzzles, follow leads and perform proto-cloak-and-dagger missions.

5. Introduce AI Through Robotics

Robotics is a hands-on way to learn about AI. Constructing a robot creates an interface for children to interact with the world, since they can easily see first-hand the results of programs that they create with an AI kit, like the LEGO Mindstorms platform or VEX robotics.

6. Host AI Competitions and Challenges

Competition, if friendly, can push young students to new learning heights and to realise just how much they've learned so far. Organise AI competitions or challenges. For example, maybe your class has mastered a form of coding. A competition (or hackathon or coding 'hack' challenge, your choice of term) can help bring it all together for some students, as they strive to program the best fun project or come up with the most interesting input to a chatbot that they've created themselves.

7. Leverage Online AI Learning Platforms

Plenty of Web portals offer AI courses and tutorials for kids, and there are many sites devoted to helping them learn coding online. There are sites like Khan Academy, Coursera and EdX that provides courses – for various skill levels – that kids can find easily by identifying their interests and grabbing the suitable course materials and adapting to their skill and interests. Many of them involve quizzes, projects or other interactive tasks that capture their attention.

8. Collaborate on AI Projects

Is learning AI really something that can be done alone? Well, largely – and that's the problem. Collaboration can help with this issue. Students should form groups to work on AI project together, whether in the classroom, as part of an after-school club, or online. Working in groups isn't just a better way of making AI learning social and enjoyable, it also encourages students to develop strengths in teamwork and communication, as well as affording students the opportunity to learn from each other, providing differing views.

9. Introduce Role Models in AI

Teachers can also draw upon role models in the field of AI to inspire further AI learning journeys of their young learners. Inviting students to learn about pioneering figures in AI's history, AI-focused leaders in the technology industry, or young innovators from India and around the world (as our interview subjects) can help students see AI through the eyes of others who have pursued it. Finally, a teacher or a school can invite guest speakers to engage their students or organise a specific virtual meetup with someone from the AI-focused industry.

10. Make AI Learning a Part of Their Interests

There is, however, the best way to bring play to AI: focus on the things that young learners are already passionate about. Does your student love sports? How about finding out what analytics are used in sports? Does she listen to music? How does AI compose music or recommend songs? Through these connections, learning is made both personal and more playful.

Conclusion: Creating a Love for AI Learning

By drawing on children's natural curiosity, creativity and interests through games, stories, robotics and collaborative projects, it's possible to turn AI from a subject often feared to one that's intriguing and rewarding.

Providing a learning environment that infuses this spirit of discovery into students' experience of AI can be the responsibility of teachers, parents and others who serve as mentors. If we achieve this, we can nurture young people who are motivated to learn and who are ready for their future lives that will increasingly centre upon AI.

CHAPTER 4

Inspiring Tomorrow's Innovators: The Role of AI in Youth Education

In every sense of the term, we live in a digital age. Artificial intelligence (AI) is transforming economies, spurring innovation, and driving growth across the globe. For today's young people, this presents an unprecedented opportunity to learn from and master AI's growth, not only to ensure future employment but also to become the creative visionaries of tomorrow. In this article, I examine the pivotal role that AI plays in today's youth education and how we can use it to inspire the next generation of creators.

The Growing Importance of AI Education

AI is a foundational technology that is touching almost every field, from healthcare and finance to entertainment and education. As AI advances, demand for technologists in the field is growing rapidly – a report claiming that AI could account for $13 trillion in global economic activity by 2030, with some of that growth coming from the next generation of AI experts.

Learning AI isn't about learning a technology, but to understand the world, and how it works, and what students can do to shape it. AI education provides the design-thinking and innovation skills that our young people need to tackle complex problems as they emerge and develop the technologies that will help solve them.

AI as a Catalyst for Innovation

One of my favourite aspects of AI is that it opens the door to creativity. AI helps solve complex problems that were considered unsolvable, from the detection of diseases to creating tailor-made learning experiences for students.

For kids, AI is a vast playground. They can be creative, try stuff, and bring their innovations to life.

If you're learning about maths in the classroom, AI can provide individually tailored support and help you build human-like cognitive skills. It can also assist in creating adaptive and interactive learning environments, and help researchers introduce emotion into learning experiences. AI technologies make learning fun and engaging, but also help students to develop human-like computational thinking skills.

Hands-On Learning: The Key to Inspiring Innovators

Enabling youth to experiment with AI in real-world applications could be a powerful way to urge these nascent innovators to embrace the technology. Here's how schools can help make AI a part of youth education:

1. AI Projects And Competitions: Give students the opportunity to participate in AI projects and competitions, where they can use their knowledge to solve real-world problems. Building a chatbot, a machine learning model, or an AI game is a good project to let your kids familiarise themselves with the concept.

2. Applying artificial intelligence within the domain of robotics: Robotics is a powerful real-world teaching medium for modern AI concepts. When students construct their own robot, then program it to perform a task, they see an immediate payoff for their work; they can observe and measure the results. For example, learners can join FIRST Robotics competitions where robotics, AI and engineering expertise is highlighted.

3. Collaborative Learning: Collaboration is the key for innovation. Encouraging students to work together on AI projects helps them to share ideas, trouble shooting and learning from each other which will not only improve the educational experience but also prepare them with the teamwork and communication skills, which is much in need in today's work force.

4. AI in Everyday Life: If you are an early adopter, get your students to notice AI in their everyday lives: what personalised suggestions do they see on Netflix? What is their smartphone 'virtual assistant' and how does it help them get things done? Students can start to imagine how they might innovate.

The Role of Educators and Mentors

Good teachers and mentors can encourage and inspire this generation of AI builders by fostering a growth mindset, encouraging curiosity, and providing students with opportunities to explore.

The other crucial element in enabling any AI to happen is to embed it in a curriculum where students feel safe to experiment and make mistakes. Innovation requires iteration and new ways of doing things, and students need possibilities to, for example, try things out, figure things out, and put things up and take them down again.

Mentoring is another great conduit for introducing students to the real world of AI. An ever-shrinking gap between tertiary institutions and work means students looking for employment face an uphill battle. Faculty members who have a finger on the employment pulse can provide valuable advice for students seeking empathy, specific expertise and a better understanding of the challenges facing the bigger picture of AI. Another good place to focus is on exposure to industry professionals.

Conclusion: Preparing Tomorrow's Innovators

AI can supercharge innovation, and the kids of today can grow up to be tomorrow's creators of AI. Through AI-powered youth education, young learners can be encouraged to pursue new concepts, develop essential skills, and contribute to the future of the technology.

As educators, parents and mentors, it is our job to give that potential a voice and a name, and a chance to become part of our innovation-rich future. Hands-on learning experiences, team projects and real-world role models could help our students unlock their creative ingenuity.

With the right education and support, there is no reason why the young people of today will not be at the forefront of this brighter future, where AI and human ingenuity work together to solve whatever problems the next generation might face.

CHAPTER 5

From Gamers to Coders: Transforming Passion into AI Skills

There are few things young people enjoy more than playing video games. What if the time spent playing were transformable into desirable skills that can pave the way for their future jobs? The world of artificial intelligence (AI) can help us tread such a path. Making creative use of young gamers' interests – let us try to transform it from gaming to game-making in a way that AI skills are built on the way.

The Link Between Gaming and AI

The relationship between gaming and AI is not as obvious as you might think at first. AI is at the core of many games, for instance as the engine that creates smart non-playing characters (NPCs), or the codes that manage difficulty levels by analysing players' behaviour. An understanding of AI should help young gamers to have a deeper understanding of how their favourite games are designed and how they could be improved.

Furthermore, because of having naturally to play against both humans and other teams of humans who are devising strategies to beat them, gamers have developed other qualities that are useful in AI: problem-solving, critical thinking and other skills such as planning and executing strategies, analysing situations briefly, calculating the likelihood of various outcomes and determining viable actions based on those factors.

Turning Gaming Passion into Coding Skills

The path from gaming to coding can be short, especially if our commitment to sound learning is placed firmly in a game. Using some of the approaches described here, young gamers can grow into coders, and coders can grow into AI creators.

1. Begin with game modding Many of today's gamers have been playing on computers since they were toddlers. Coding for their age group has the perfect training ground: the easily modifiable game. Modding – modification of existing games – is an easy step into coding that is already familiar and fun. Games such as Minecraft and Skyrim offer modding engines that let players modify gameplay, design new levels, even write new rules of the game. This kind of experience starts a player on the path of coding and provides an entrée to more difficult programming.

2. Try Game Development Platforms: There are several free game development platforms such as Unity and Unreal Engine that are widely used by professional game developers and offer free play-around versions for beginners. Utilising these platforms, one can create games from scratch and get a hands-on experience of coding and AI development, which otherwise can be a bit blunt, because the immediate impact of code is not visible. Furthermore, it can be one of the most beneficial and motivating ways to learn for an aspiring young programmer.

3. Compete in Game Jams: Game jams force participants to build a game from conception to completion in 24- to 48-hour marathon events. These provide a chance for young gamers to apply their coding skills in a group setting and a super-charged social environment. Many jams feature the development of a game around a theme, challenging participants to be creative and try new things with their coding and AI skills.

4. Apply AI Through Game Programming: Once young learners become more comfortable with programming conventions, they might take it a step further and include AI in their games. For example, they might want to program NPCs to respond and behave in a more realistic manner, create AI-driven decision-making routines, or even create more adaptive experiences for the game play. Online courses and tutorials geared toward AI within games can provide learners with the required knowledge and skills they need to proceed.

The Benefits of Combining Gaming with AI Learning

Learning AI skills through play can generate a slew of rewards that go way beyond learning to code itself. When passions for gaming are fuelled by emerging competencies, the road to both passion and mastery opens for the player.

1. Problem-Solving Skills: Both gaming and AI development require building complex solutions to problems – and building games offers learners the chance to practise this skill in a way that feels natural and fun.

2. Added Motivation to Learn: Any learning activity is more appealing if it's facilitated around something the student is passionate about. Gamers will have lots of motivation to learn AI and coding if that makes it possible for them to create their own games or improve existing ones.

3. Portfolio of Projects: As students build their own games and AI projects, they build a portfolio, which can be used to show future employers or to apply to more advanced educational opportunities. This portfolio may be evidence of not only technical skills, but imagination and inventiveness as well.

4. Teaching skills for future careers: The gaming industry is one of the largest and fastest-growing sectors in the world and it constantly requires new AI developers. Thus, by combining gaming and AI, young students prepare themselves for some interesting careers in a field they consider as their interest.

Encouraging the Transition from Player to Creator

Parents, teachers and mentors can start helping the gamer cross the bridge to coder:

1. Give them a means: Make sure the right tools and resources are available: game development environments, coding courses, AI learning materials (many of which are free to use or very cheap).

2. Foster a Learning Environment for Experimentation: Encourage curious exploration and experimentation. Let students get it wrong because the value lies in learning from the trial. Celebrate their successes — whether finishing a code tutorial, creating a simple game or embedding an AI in a project.

3. Engage With Peers: Encourage your teen to get involved in online forums, code clubs or game-dev clubs as having like-minded peers to learn with can be highly motivating. It also provides opportunities for feedback, peer evaluation and social support.

4. School Career Opportunities: Help students understand school career opportunities in game development and AI. Share guest-speaker stories from industry partners, successes, and pathways to careers.

Conclusion: Empowering the Next Generation of AI Innovators

The path from gamer to AI coder leads through the playground of the mind, and its possibilities are thrilling. 'It's a perfectly natural path to go from gaming to making AI,' says Shlaer. 'You could turn what we consider an avocational obsession into a vocational obsession.

But, with the right kind of nurturing, support, resources and encouragement, those current day gamers of all different ages can, over time, become the overall gaming innovators of tomorrow delivering more of what is needed not only in gaming but in our larger futures thanks to the outreach of AI. When all's said and done, the future of AI can be bright, and in leveraging their already well-known love of gaming, we can help more youth chart a path toward becoming the next generation of AI leaders.

CHAPTER 6

AI for All: Breaking Down Barriers for Young Learners

One thing is undeniable: AI education is already transforming the worlds of medicine, education, finance, entertainment and almost every industry. Yet, many young learners lack access to quality AI education. For some, it may be as simple as the perceived lack of availability of materials and programmes that foster interest in AI. Some others may not have adequate access to computers or tools to get a hands-on experience. Some may think it is a subject for the elites, no doubt influenced by others' perceptions that AI is unattainable – too technical, too complicated, off-limits. How do we remove these barriers to ensure quality AI education for young learners, regardless of their background or situation?

Understanding the Barriers to AI Education

This essay on navigating AI education barriers and promoting responsible and innovative practice among young learners tackles the issue by looking at what these barriers are and how they manifest.

1. Lack of access to technology: One of the biggest barriers is not having access to the technology. Many students (especially those from poor or rural communities) do not have access to computers or the internet required to experiment with AI. For some, this would literally strand them on the wrong side of the digital divide: area divides where learners can't get to the learning resources or engage in online courses or coding communities.

2. Insufficient Exposure to STEM Education: STEM (Science, Technology, Engineering, Mathematics) education may be underfunded or devalued in many schools, especially in underserved communities, which results in insufficient exposure to concepts related to AI as well as to technology careers.

3. The AI is mysterious and difficult to grasp: The field of AI is considered very technical, complex and math-oriented; this can scare away young learners well before they have even considered the field as a specialisation. Students from different backgrounds, especially those who do not consider themselves 'tech-savvy' or have difficulties with maths or sciences, are less motivated to engage with AI as they do not feel that they would fit in or be successful.

4. Gender and cultural stereotypes: Gender and cultural stereotypes are also a factor in deterring young learners from considering AI. For instance, girls and underrepresented minorities may feel that AI and other technology careers are not 'for them', because they either cannot picture themselves or someone like them in a senior AI role, or because of societal expectations or cultural biases.

Strategies for Breaking Down Barriers:

All young learners should have the opportunity to study AI at school, and the constraints described above should be removed to create an inclusive learning environment.

1. Broaden access to technology: Fostering access to technology is paramount. Offering affordable devices, aiding in network connectivity in underserved areas and funding technology grants or scholarships to students in need are among the feasible ways to open the door to AI education. School and community learning hubs are also an option. For instance, computer labs can be created at schools and community centres to enhance access to AI technologies.

2. Embedding AI in the Curriculum: Since AI is not central to any other science thread, the main way an embodiment in the curriculum can be realised is to embed elements of AI in that curriculum. This approach would make AI more widely available to all students than an approach centred on a single, AI-specific thread. The embedded AI would not themselves be sufficient to support students to learn computational thinking, but it would support students in taking an AI lens to develop their mathematical and scientific understanding. AI was competently integrated into the final years of schooling in Turkey (up to and including Year 12) through computer science courses that took an embodied AI approach rather than focusing on the mathematical machinery alone. This approach would mean that, for the purposes of the curriculum, for instance, numbers could be thought of in terms of representations that are manipulated by students undertaking the study of mathematics. Embedding would include activities such as maths, science and computer science projects or activities that incorporate AI learning.

3. Creating Inclusive Learning Environments: Making every classroom an innovative place to learn by encouraging all students to consider AI, such as through using inclusive language, removing stereotypes and unconscious bias, and providing needed support for students who might be struggling to understand the basics of AI. Teachers can showcase diverse role models in the field of AI, including more female and minority role models, to help all students recognise that they can also become AI leaders.

4. Making Resources Free and Accessible: There exist plenty of free and accessible resources available for students to learn AI for free, irrespective of their background. Some of the existing open-source AI courses and tutorials are available on platforms like Code.org, Khan Academy and Coursera. Additionally, open-source tools and software such as Python, TensorFlow and Scratch allow children to experiment with AI without having to buy costly equipment or get licences for their software.

Having access to these resources would eliminate financial obstacles and open an AI education to all.

5. Sowing the Seeds of Mentorship and Support Networks: Mentorship can help dismantle many of the barriers to learning AI. Students who can access mentors to identify resources, provide motivation and encouragement, will be better supported in their AI education. Schools, community organisations, as well as online avenues can engage mentors to foster connections between students and professionals working in AI. Students can also support each other in a sense of community where they can collaborate, share, and learn from peers.

6. Making AI Awesome Again: Another way to de-mystify AI is to push back on the narrative that it is too difficult, or that only certain kinds of students can be engaged in it. You can do this by breaking down AI concepts to their smallest components, keeping it light and simple, and linking AI to concepts that are easily comprehensible. For instance, it's important to give clear, real-world examples of people using AI in their daily lives. At the same time, teachers should emphasise that AI is a creative, problem-solving field that involves critical thinking. It is a field that may resonate, and in which students can excel. All this points toward a higher goal: reshaping the narrative around AI.

Conclusion: AI for All

As our futures are increasingly likely to be shaped by artificial intelligence that more and more denote 'human-like' capabilities, it would be a shame to deprive young learners of what could be a world-changing technology. Considering this, it is important to tear down institutional, financial and pedagogical barriers to student access of AI, and give all students equal opportunities to engage with

AI, to develop relevant skills, and to perhaps forge a future career in AI.

We, as educators, parents and mentors, have the duty to create a welcoming environment that empowers all students to learn AI by providing technology access, incorporating AI into the curriculum, fostering diversity and inclusion, and providing mentorship and resources.

Whether or not the future of AI belongs to all of us will depend on the students and trainees of today, and with inclusive and accessible AI education we can all stand a chance to unleash our ingenuity and prepare to make a stand in this artificial world.

CHAPTER 7

The Digital Playground: How to Make AI Learning Exciting for Kids

Artificial intelligence (AI) is one of the most exciting developments in technology right now — with the potential to transform not just healthcare but our entertainment experiences as well. But when it comes time to combining AI and kids, making it as fun and easy to learn as the video games, apps and other content that kids love requires us to innovate. The magic formula is for AI learning to be a digital playground — a game-like, exploratory environment, where AI learning objectives are embedded within a user experience (UX) that's as fun and immersive as the games kids play now.

The Appeal of the Digital Playground

Children are digital natives, growing up in a world that affords their curiosity and innate sensibilities to be awakened by technology as an integral part of living, breathing and learning – hence it is exactly the right habitat in which to germinate some seeds that will bloom into those 'AI flowers'. The image of a digital playground here taps into their curiosity to interact with the digital world in a playful way, making learning about AI a rewarding, enjoyable experience.

Creating a Fun and Interactive Learning Environment

To make AI learning stick, it must be turned into an environment that fosters exploration, imagination and play for kids. Here are a handful of suggestions to pantify AI education:

1. Gamify your child's learning environment: Your child's educational environment can be gamified so that learning about AI is no different than playing one. Consider the growing number of game-like platforms that teach participants a wide variety of AI skills. For example,

Lightbot (which I will refer to frequently in this article) is a lightbot that requires players to guide it to pressing specific controls. Others, such as CodeCombat and Tynker, teach programming and coding fundamentals using game-like environments in which players must solve puzzles, 'win' levels, and receive rewards if they succeed.

2. Start with Coding Games: Coding is the foundation of all AI. Luckily, there are a ton of excellent, interactive coding games geared toward kids. For instance, Scratch, from MIT, teaches theory and logic-based thinking by allowing young coders to program and animate games and puzzles by dragging and dropping blocks of code. They can share their creations online and download games made by other users. (Best of all, Scratch comes in more than 40 languages, so there is something for everyone.) Another great tool is Blockly, developed by Google with different apps for various age groups, such as ScratchJr, designed especially for preschoolers to use with parents or teachers. There are also age-appropriate coding games available in the Apple app store, Google Play and elsewhere, such as Hopscotch. As children build projects, they learn the basic elements of coding along with theory and logic-based thinking.

3. Play With Robots and AI Toys: Robotics and AI playthings provide a tactile, physical play experience to allow kids to interact with AI. Some existing products involving LEGO Mindstorms, Dash and Dot, and Cozmo have been created offer children exposure to robotics and AI through play. With these toys, kids can build and programme robots and interact with them using touch. These robots utilise sensors, algorithms and machine learning to learn more about the world.

4. Nurture Creative AI Projects: Creative media-making is a useful expression of learning and an entirely human thing to do; AI presents joyous prospects for creative projects and challenges. Urge kids to look for things they can do in this realm: can they design a video game with an AI game-maker toolset? Or build a drawing tool? Or compose digital music with AI? Combining AI with creative expression spurs creativity and helps children form useful perceptions about how this technology might be used.

5. Make use of AI-powered educational apps: Parents can take advantage of various apps that utilise AI to aid their children in gaining conceptual ideas by directly interacting with them. Whether it is math or music, neuroscience indicates that the younger a child is, the greater the opportunity for leveraging their innate curiosity and auditory representations of sounds. Apps such as DreamBox, Squirrel AI and Photomath make use of machine learning to personalise learning by taking cues from a child's learning style and pace, adapting lessons and constructive feedback on the spot. By incorporating AI-powered chatbots and other exercises through games and real-time feedback loops, these apps can make the learning experience more fun for the child.

6. Use AI As a Medium for Storytelling: Using storytelling to understand complex ideas is quintessential to children's cognitive process. Moreover, allowing them to have richer and age-appropriate narratives with a revamped plot will help them make sense of the purpose of AI. For digital tools to translate the abstract concept of AI into narratives, it may be an imperative to cultivate a culture where AI is seen as an opportunity rather than a threat to job automation. Moreover, using AI as a medium for storytelling will help reap benefits of richer, age-appropriate narratives capable of alleviating and mitigating children's fear of AI. In this premise, learning with AI can incorporate richer and immersive narratives while engaging children with a haptic interface.

Making AI Learning Accessible

As children engage in the digital playground, taking ownership of their learning through the AI playfield, they will encounter accessibility and affordability issues. It is up to us to ensure that all children, regardless of socioeconomic background, could engage with these resources. Here are some ideas for democrtising AI education:

1. Make Resources Available That Are Free and Low Cost: There are numerous free and low-cost learning resources available to today's kids. Many of the most popular coding sites such as Code.org, Khan Academy and Coursera offer free AI and coding courses, with Code.org even promising free computer-science classes for every student. Many of the coding platforms and AI toys on the market also offer free trial periods or lower cost versions of the toys that can make them available to a wide swath of children.

2. Provide after-school learning opportunities: Provide children with access to technology and AI learning resources at community centres, libraries or after-school programmes like Girls Who Code or Black Girls Code. Many of these programmes can be completed from home, but with supervision, making them easier to synchronise. In situations where not all students have devices or access to the internet in their homes, centres could offer workshops, coding clubs and AI-related activities where children could learn and have a rich social experience of working with AI.

3. Involve the Parents: Parents are crucial to their child's learning journey. So, ask parents to explore websites related to AI with their child, to engage in hobbies that use coding, and to foster a loving attitude about technology. Wouldn't AI learning be more fun if parents participate with their children? Then kids will understand AI and love it and won't be afraid of it.

4. Make AI Role Models Visible: Representation is important in inspiring children and seeing role models who look or sound like them can be truly enjoyable. Showcase role models in AI – women, Black individuals, immigrants, people from any underrepresented communities – and anyone else working in AI. Displaying that one can be ANYBODY to pursue their interest in AI can attract more children.

Conclusion: The Joy of Learning Through Play

Given the seemingly limitless possibilities of AI – and by making it into a digital playground, learning AI can become a source of joy and discovery for children. With the use of gamification, arts-based projects, robotics and stories, we can help children discover AI in their lives.

Instead, we educators, parents and mentors should help turn the classroom or room into a stage where learning becomes play, where it's fun to discover, where new connections are made eased by AI learning tools and applications that are interactive and fun, and where young people are not only inspired to take interest in the wonders of AI, but also empowered to become digital makers, innovators and ready to embrace a future that may be radically reshaped by AI.

In this digital playground, we can have fun while cultivating the practical, cognitive, and interpersonal skills necessary to ride the tidal wave of AI that we're currently engendering.

CHAPTER 8

Why Every Young Person Should Learn AI: A Parent's Guide

With the pace of technological change speeding up to an unprecedented extent, a question parents battle with is not whether new technology (such as AI) will impact the futures of their children, but how to equip them for success in an AI-driven world. This article aims to be a parent's guide to why every young person should learn AI, and how she can help her child become part of this emerging world.

The Growing Importance of AI

Everyone is feeling the AI fever: we get recommendations from our streaming services, Siri answers some of our questions, and Alexa keeps track of our schedule. As AI is evolving, it is not only evolving, but also already here and influencing every single one of us in every single aspect of our social and individual lives: healthcare, education, finance, transportation, and more.

Learning AI makes perfect sense for today's youth because practical experience of the technology of the future encourages an interest and skill in the coding that will underpin our growing technological future. AI would also present a world of creativity, innovation and problem-solving for today's children. The coding skills will become second nature to the young computer-literate age.

The Benefits of Learning AI Early

From the very beginning, by initiating children into AI, there are far-reaching advantages in addition to teaching them how to code:

1. Teaching critical thinking and problem-solving: Learning AI involves mastering the techniques used to analyse data and find patterns that help solve real-world problems. This skill in critical thinking and problem-solving can be very helpful in any field that a child might grow up to choose.

2. Encouraging Creativity and Innovation: AI is a creativity generator: AI can be used by the kids to design new technologies, develop apps and create their own games. Children can experiment and play with AI to make their ideas tangible and bring their creativity to life. Kids will develop innovative thinking that will lead them to become entrepreneurs.

3. Learning AI When Young Could Launch a Great Career At present, job openings for AI workers vastly outnumber those with relevant qualifications to fill them, and this employment gap is growing every year. The earlier children can get a start on AI learning, the stronger a foundation they'll have for AI careers, whether they go into AI directly.

4. Modelling a Growth Mindset: Learning with AI can be hard, but it also creates opportunity for learning and growing. As kids struggle through thorny problems and learn new skills, they build confidence for taking on more challenges and developing a growth mindset – a key for success in life.

How Parents Can Support AI Learning

You as a parent are key in nurturing your child's development as they enter the AI world. So here are some straightforward, achievable things that you can do: 1. Encourage them to participate in computational thinking activities.

1. Start young, with AI concepts: sit your kid down and introduce them to the very basics of the field in an age-appropriate way. You don't have to be an AI expert to do this; there's plenty of material out there to help you get started. If they're young, try a story, or a game that involves AI. If they're older, there are plenty of beginner-friendly coding platforms (such as Scratch or Code.org) that get their feet wet, and even reach the shores of AI.

2. Give Time and Freedom for Play and Discovery: You don't need to hurry your child into enthusiastically embracing the latest AI technology. You won't be able to stop them anyway, so your role here is usually one of guidance and support. Give them time to play and explore at their own pace, and then encourage a range of projects from building a simple chatbot to programming a game to tinkering with robotics sets. Show them that it's OK to mess up sometimes, and frame system failures and false positives (or even negatives) as inevitable while you learn from setbacks and failures. The key goals here are curiosity, a love of learning, and the freedom to continue to take such risks.

3. Give them Tools and Opportunities: Many resources are available for children to learn AI, including free courses, tutorials, coding sites, and AI toys. Ensure that your kid has access to them and give them the space to explore what works best for them. Finally, enrol them in robotics camps, AI workshops or after-school coding programmes.

4. Encourage Learning Environment: Set up an encouraging environment for learning AI for kids by celebrating all their small achievements and rewarding the child with positive reinforcements. Let the child be aware that learning AI is the process of trial and error, not just one that can be learnt overnight.

5. Meet and Mingle with Peers: Encourage your child to connect with peers who are also interested in AI concepts. This could be in the form of meetups at coding clubs, in cyber spaces via online forums, or in-person within communities of learners or makers. The process of learning with peers can be a great motivator for your child, and serves as an important opportunity for collaborative practice, idea-sharing, and feedback.

6. Showcase Role Models and Career Paths: show them who is a role model in AI, from tech leaders to entrepreneurs and young innovators. Talk about job opportunities in AI and how the skills can be applied in different fields; show your child the possibilities in the field.

Addressing Common Concerns

Finally, you might be a concerned parent, worried that your child will learn AI. (You might even not know yourself what AI is.) Here are some questions that parents often have, and thoughtful replies to the question.

1. 'AI is too hard to learn for my child.' To be clear, AI is complex, but there are many excellent resources that take it back to the fundamentals, giving the concepts in simple terms and step-by-step instructions.

2. 'I'm not technical, so I don't know how my child is doing' You don't need to understand the inner workings of your child's tech life to support it. Your time is better served on encouraging, resourcing and letting your child explore. Importantly, everyone needs help sometimes. You can leverage the army of helpful people online, in forums and support websites. If your child does have a question, they can always ask you to Google it.

3. 'I'm worried about screen time.' As with any hobby, activity or topic, AI learning should be balanced with other activities. If your child is on chatGPT for hours at a time – or is starting to come across as a chatGPT itself – give them a kick outside. Encourage them to take a well-deserved break, embrace physical activity, or explore AI as a topic of interest rather than something to spew out of them.

Conclusion: Preparing for the Future

It is all too fast for you to keep up with. The world is slowly but surely leaving you behind. The only force in the world that will master the coming changes before they hit us is AI – that's Artificial Intelligence in case Mum stopped you half-way and told you. I am a machine recommending you teach your child to learn AI and not only equip him with skills for business careers, but also teach him the skills he will need to tackle everything in life.

You'll tap into their innate curiosity about AI. Doing this alone might seem daunting: providing resources, creating a space for them and linking them to other kids who share this interest. But once you get started, you'll realise that these actions will not only cultivate your children thrive in an AI world but will have a tremendous impact on their lives at all stages.

In the end, the person prepared to take advantage of and contribute to the field of AI will be the most successful – which is why it is imperative to arm your child with the skills to harness the power of this technology. By teaching your child how to communicate with AI, you are setting them up for a bright and prosperous future.

CHAPTER 9

AI and the Youth: Building the Innovators of the Future

The world is about to experience a technological revolution, and artificial intelligence (AI) is at the heart of it. Understanding AI and using it to solve real-world problems will play a crucial role for this generation before it takes over. UK students look at various screens. Picture courtesy Claire Burrows/Panos Photos/Getty ImagesAsk very young children what they want to be when they grow up and one of the first places, they'll say they want to work is at 'Disneyland'. As they get a bit older, divergent interests emerge: a self-professed tomboy, for instance, exclaims she wants to be a basketball player. Then others chime in, saying they want to work in hospitals or specialise in art or design, such as 'Ornaments' and 'Bakers'. In senior school, my students will want to be medical doctors, physicists, astronomers, geographers or environmental activists. Many of them express a desire to become the president of the United States, while others are serious about training to become professional athletes. These career aspirations fascinate me. I often ponder where 'Disneyland' would be on my career map, or whether there's some concept of a metaphorical 'Disneyland' for my former students. But before I can even begin to unpack this further, a student interrupts me, reminding me that Lisa Frank, the artist behind many school supplies, is not someone who works at Disneyland. 'T I acknowledge, but I invite her to contemplate how the things we imagine and aspire to, especially in childhood, inform and shape our future realities. 'That's actually a great question, Ms Lin,' she replies, with a smile. She shares that she wants to be an environmental engineer to 'help the world'.

Why AI Education is Crucial for the Next Generation

It's no longer about future AI, as AI is already stepping into the real world in many fields including health care, financial services, education and entertainment. AI is also inspiring advances in new areas and opening new opportunities. You will also learn the reason why you – the new generation – need to study AI subjects. It is not just about your future job, but also about how you can become the co-builder of the future technologies.

Here are some key reasons why AI education is crucial for the next generation:

1. Getting Ready for Future Careers: As AI evolves, the need for professionals in the domain of AI and related areas is rising exponentially. According to a World Economic Forum report, AI and machine learning are among the top emerging professions. Learning AI enables youth to be ready to work in these highly demanded profiles and get ahead in the competitive jobs market in the future.

2. Fostering Innovation and Creativity: AI is a powerful force that can help innovate and create. Students who learn AI could come up with new technologies, solve real-world problems, and push the envelope of what's achievable with their ideas. Students can also explore their creativity in the comfort of classrooms.

3. Tackling global problems: The world is facing many challenges, from climate action and healthcare to inequality and education. AI can help to address many of these challenges by giving us new insights, boosting efficiency and enabling better decisions. By teaching young people AI skills today, we will help them build solutions that can tackle these issues tomorrow.

4. The Growth Mindset: Learning high-level AI requires critical and creative thinking as well as determination. The more difficult AI projects that young people work on, the more they acquire a growth mindset: the belief that my ability and intelligence can improve by learning and effort. This has been shown to be a solid foundation for success in any discipline – and a valuable attribute for any student to acquire.

Strategies for Building the Innovators of the Future

If we want to raise the next generation of innovators, we must be sure that we give ourselves, our young people and our communities ready access to the tools, resources and support we need so that we can learn and apply AI. So, what can we all do? Here's a few ideas:

1. AI should become part of the curriculum from the bottom: fundamentals of AI should be incorporated into school curricula. For example, this could be done by adding machine-learning portions to mathematics, science or even computer-science courses. Another approach is to assign AI-related course projects or activities.

2. Encourage Making by Learning: Making should be included in the list because having hands-on learning experience is important for understanding of AI. Students should engage in learning by doing regardless of the level they're at (e.g., making project with a simple chatbot; create a machine learning application; design an AI app). Hands-on learning will shape a student's perspective of AI, and they will understand where AI is going by gaining actual experiences.

3. Encourage Collaboration and Teamwork: Collaboration is essential for innovation, and students should work together on AI projects. The reason for this is because having peers to work with can help students share different ideas, work through problems that arise from each other's thoughts, and build each other's understanding of the information they learn together. This helps students become more well-rounded learners, and better prepared to work as a team in the workplace.

4. Make AI Resources Available: Many AI resources are now available online for free: tutorials and courses, sourced-code libraries, AI-based learning aids, easy-to-access development platforms, etc. AI education in schools, community organisations and libraries can make such resources available to students.

5. Feature AI Role Models: Representation in AI is critical. Providing young people with examples of role models pursuing the field can encourage students to see themselves as being a part of their own AI learning journey. Share with your students the disparate experiences of individuals who have varied roles in AI and contributed to the field; whether it's tech leaders, entrepreneurs or young innovators. By providing role models, you can help students begin to believe that an area like AI is accessible to them.

The Role of Educators, Parents, and Mentors

Educators, parents and mentors, schooled in a growth mindset – and presented with ways to think, talk and act this way – can encourage their interest in AI, prepare them to grasp it, and position them to succeed.

Here are some ways to support young people in their AI learning journey:

1. Provide a creative and collaborative: Reassure students while they are experimenting with AI, helping them see the opportunities to make mistakes and re-try, and celebrating their successes. Applaud their achievements and support perseverance through challenges.

2. Pair Students with a Mentor: AI learning can be enhanced through mentorship, which can provide support and guidance. Pairing students with a mentor can enable them to benefit from the experience of individuals who are familiar with the ins and outs of AI and can provide them with the extra support and encouragement needed to learn it. Mentors can also help students understand how to navigate the intricacies of AI and give them advice on the best career pathways.

3. Promote a Lifetime of Learning: Admittedly, the speed at which this research is evolving is such that there is literally no way that a single lesson or course could possibly cover all that information, not to mention technologies that have not yet been invented. Consequently, promoting lifelong learning for students is very important in an instant learning/research age because staying curious, seeking out new learning opportunities and keeping up to date with today's fast-moving AI environment could help students keep ahead of this changing field and continue innovating over the remainder of their lifetime.

Conclusion: Empowering the Innovators of Tomorrow

By preparing students to learn how to learn AI – not to be tested on it, but to master it – we will allow this technology to transform the world. As futurist Ray Kurzweil said: 'Genius breaks the mould. The trouble with these geniuses is they are maladjusted to society.' So, for the genius leaders to emerge and transform society, society and its education reformers must adapt.

Alongside our roles as educators, parents and mentors, this potential is something that we need to nurture and help them to realise: to develop the skills, capabilities and mindset to thrive in the AI-powered world to come. The future beckons, and with the appropriate education and preparation, young people can lead the way into a world where AI and human creativity meet and support each other to overcome the problems that lie ahead.

CHAPTER 10

Nurturing Curiosity: How AI Can Spark a Lifelong Love of Learning

It's also the first step into a vast world of learning and discovery. Curiosity, when channelled, is both the motor and the energy that powers learning. It can be the springboard into a life of intellectual exploration – a sense of wonder that remains unscathed by formal, academic education. In the increasingly complex and technologically saturated modern world, the nurturing of curiosity in young people is more important than ever before. Artificial intelligence (AI) can play a significant role in stimulating and fostering curiosity among young people so that they may develop a life-long thirst for learning, which is the wellspring of unlimited potential.

The Role of Curiosity in Learning

Curiosity is a key aspect of human nature: a field of investigation that cries out to be explored. Of all the virtues, curiosity is perhaps the most important one for learning. It motivates us to seek out new information, develop new experiences and skills, and try new things. Students who are curious are more likely to be independent learners, more highly motivated, and more resilient in the face of setbacks.

But in regular schools and other educational settings, it can be squashed by the confines of curriculums, tests and assessments, and other forms of learning that primarily promote rote memorisation. One way to nurture curiosity is to provide learning environments where exploration,

creativity and enquiry can run free. School will be truly useful and effective when it exploits more than just AI; it can do wonders with a human touch.

How AI Can Spark Curiosity

AI can engage young learners with new avenues for investigating, making and discovering – here are some examples of how:

1. Interactive learning experiences: We create interactive learning experiences that engage the learner and bring concepts alive. Consider self-directed learning through AI-powered educational apps. Adaptive educational apps that can change as a student learns give the student a suitable learning experience based on their learning style and pace, such as does this learning style make more sense to the student. Learners can now experience concepts in more fun ways and interact with a medium to engage with the concept.

2. Use of Real-World Problems: In AI, students can explore real-world problems and solve them using technology. In subjects like healthcare, environmental science and social justice, students can utilise AI to comb through vast amounts of data to find patterns and make predictions. Students could see how AI can help to solve problems in the world around them and gain a sense of how technology can address real issues.

3. Creative AI Projects: Creativity and forward-thinking curiosity go together, and AI opens unending possibilities for creative exploration through new games, graphics and visual art, and music, among countless other creative pursuits. Experimenting with the use of AI empowers students to experiment with and discover their own interests and passions, ultimately fostering a deep love of learning and creativity for years to come.

4. Scallop 1: Hands-on learning Hands-on learning is vital in aptitude-spotting, and our AI will allow children to learn about things hands-on, and with AI too. How? They can build, code and program robots directly, they can design and build their AI applications, and they can do data science with real datasets.

Strategies for Nurturing Curiosity with AI

To inspire curiosity and a lifelong love of learning, people who teach, parent and otherwise serve the roles of mentor can use the following strategies.

1. Open for Inquiry-Based Learning: Inquiry-based learning is a student-centred form of learning which focuses on inciting students with questions, enables them to explore the topic, and kindle their interest to answer the queries. This could be a nice way to combine AI learning – the students could pose a question related to the topic and concept and use AI tools to research the topic, visualise/analyse data, and create a solution for their concerns. Let the students ask questions about anything they find interesting around the world and make use of AI as a tool.

2. Provide a Secure Space for Learning: find secure ways for students to explore ideas and learn through genuine enquiry. Create an environment that encourages students to take risks, make mistakes and learn from them. Positively reinforce their successes, no matter how small.

3. Make AI Part of Everyday Learning: Exploit AI and make it a regular part of everyday learning, including across subjects and in activities. For example, use AI in lessons or activities across math, science, language arts, and social studies. Demonstrate easy AI-related tools that affect our daily lives, including virtual assistants, recommendation systems, and self-driving cars. When AI becomes part of their learning as a matter of course, this may reinforce the idea that 'AI' is relevant in ways that matter to students.

4. Let Them Explore AI Independently: Allow students to explore AI independently by providing access to coding platforms, AI-powered educational apps, online tutorials, and open-source AI tools. By letting them go down technology rabbit holes, you can help students develop a sense of ownership over their learning and ignite a lifelong love of discovery.

5. Show role models and success stories: By showing students role models and success stories about using AI in the real world, students will be inspired to pursue their own passions and dreams. Highlight how some students or young individuals with an interest in AI, either as tech-entrepreneurs or academic researchers, have become vocal leaders and successfully improved students' experiences through research or even inspired more students to study and create AI. Show them what's possible.

Conclusion: Cultivating a Lifelong Love of Learning

Because curiosity is one of the sparks of a lifetime of learning – not knowing but seeking to know – AI can foster learning with young people through interactive learning and digital play, inquiry-based learning experiences, and creative exploration. These are the opportunities to make AI come to life for children and enable a love of discovery.

We as teachers, parents and mentors can create a space where curiosity can grow by bringing AI into everyday learning, providing students with access to resources and role models, and encouraging curiosity within students' learning environments.

The future is wide open, and by promoting interest in and prompting curiosity using AI, we can encourage the next generation to dream up new possibilities, solve complex issues and shape the world of tomorrow.

CHAPTER 11

Coding is Cool: How to Get Young People Excited About AI

Coding is a gateway skill to limitless possibilities, including the opportunity to build artificial intelligence (AI) bots. As a technologist, I see tremendous benefits to introducing kids to coding and AI early on. But it seems that making kids passionate about coding and AI is a hard sell, especially if they see it as hard, boring and not for them. The answer lies in leveraging their interests, making it fun, and showing applications in the real world.

Why Coding Matters

Coding is the lingua franca – the universal language – the cornerstone of the digital world. Without it, we could not access websites or apps, play video games or use artificial intelligence! By learning to code, students gain the ability to conceive, create, and solve challenges in a tech-driven world.

Here are some reasons why coding is a valuable skill for young people:

1. Creative empowerment: Young people can empower themselves by creating their own experiences online, whether it's creating the content of a website, the rules of a game, or the functionality of an app. It's from experience that they can become empowered creators – the feeling that 'I can do that' is hugely motivating for young people when they see things unfold based on their own ideas through code onscreen.

2. Groundwork for Future Jobs: From software development and data science to artificial intelligence and robotics, the need for people with coding skills is on the rise, and it's anticipated to remain that way for some time.

Learning to code prepares young people for a whole host of future jobs.

3. Logic, problem solving and perseverance: Learning how to code leads to better logic and problem solving. As children work on coding challenges, they learn these skills. They also learn grit, which is what psychologists call perseverance. The ability to problem solves and persevere through difficulties is what we help foster at Kano.

4. Better understanding of the world: As technology becomes more central to the world, learning how it works is crucial to better understand and participate in the digital world, and be an informed and active citizen.

Strategies for Making Coding Cool

If parents or teachers want youth to learn about coding and AI, it is crucial to make it fun, interesting and exciting for them. The following are several methods to achieve this.

1. Link Coding to Something They Rather Like The best way to make coding cool is to link it to something that the child likes. Like if they like video games, show them the possibility of using a game development platform such as Unity or Roblox to code and create a game. Or if they are into music, teach them how coding can help to compose music or write an app on music. Anything really.

2. Use Gamification: Gamification is another way of making coding fun: two steps beyond edutainment. A whole suite of products uses game-like environments as a way of teaching about coding (eg, CodeCombat, Lightbot, Tynker). Students can proceed through challenges, win points, and rise as a hero (or another role) when they level up. In short, the educational process feels like playing a game – not a classroom or laboratory thing at all.

3. Make it Hands-On: The most important element of making coding cool is (ironically!) physical. Projects are how students get to use their coding for something cool, directly relevant and applicable to the real world. Projects give kids a way to apply their coding skills and make them more invested in learning the language. Whether it's building a website or app to share with their friends, or even creating an animation or mix tape, hands-on experiences show students how they can use coding to make something real. It also serves as a nice reward for practicing their coding skills, since students love to show off projects they have completed.

4. Encourage Coding into AI How to implement: Encourage students to give AI a try by embedding some AI related projects in the coding program. This will help students understand how AI is developed through coding – and how they can use their coding skills to do so. Introduce AI using coding projects like writing a chatbot, creating a machine learning model, or programming a robot. How it helps – AI is one of the hottest fields in technology when it comes to maximising creativity and driving possibility. Students who become familiar with AI through coding can make a strong case for using their skills in crafting state-of-the-art technologies.

5. Demonstrate Role Models and Success Stories: Exposing students to real-world examples of coding and AI in action dares them to embark on their own coding journey. The good news is that there is an abundance of great stories about tech entrepreneurs, iOS game developers or just young coders making a difference. Don't be shy to share these with your students – if you can entice them to learn more about the topic by piquing their interest with stories about what's possible through coding, all the better! (If you need some inspiration, check out the success stories on code.org.)

Encouraging a Growth Mindset in Coding

Teaching someone to code isn't easy, but learning to embrace a growth mindset (in which you believe that ability and intelligence are a result of deliberate effort and study) is just as important as any coding lesson. Here are five ways that coders of all ages can learn a growth mindset.

1. Praising Process: Iterate, iterate, iterate This means praising all the stages of the process. So instead of focusing only on getting the output right ('Well done, you have the same shape!'), celebrate what went into the effort and the progress that students are making. This could be the 'output' but could also include things such as: 'Well done for trying something new', 'Well done for taking a chance', or 'Well done for sticking at something until you got it right (eventually)!' 1.

2. Let them experiment: Let them try coding as many little programming projects as they feel like, even if they don't know in advance how to make them work. Tell them that even if they're taking the software on mysterious little detours, 'mistakes' are part of what makes the learning experience worthwhile, and that the power of making 'mistakes' is that every single one of them is an opportunity to learn.

3. Offer Opportunities for Collaboration: Coding can be more fun and less intimidating if approached as a group activity. Offer students opportunities to work together on coding projects, for instance, in coding clubs, or in other online forums or group activities. Coding projects help students to express their ideas, generate confidence in the computing process, and gain insights from their peers.

Conclusion: Making Coding a Lifelong Passion

Learning how to code can create a world of opportunities for young people – from having the power to invent their own digital experiences, to teaching themselves new skills, or even joining nascent companies pioneering groundbreaking technologies (such as AI) and working on projects that will shape the future. Culture has the power to make things cool, and if we make coding cool, then young people will begin exploring the technology in front of them, and see if it becomes a hobby, pastime and passion for life.

It's up to all us educators, parents and mentors to design learning environments that make coding fun, engaging and relevant. We can bolster our students' excitement about coding by connecting lessons to students' interests, including elements of gamification, using hands-on projects and showcasing coding role models. By making coding fun and inclusive, perhaps soon we'll be able to add another item to the ever-growing task list and title for the vital (and often overlooked) founders of society – parent, family liaison, technology handler and chief coder.

The future is digital. If we teach today's youngsters how to code, we're positioning them to succeed in a mainstream adopting technology as its core headed for world domination. The kids are tech-friendly, and we can help them embrace innovation.

CHAPTER 12

AI Adventures: Fun Projects to Get Kids Hooked on Technology

Just like there was a space race in the mid 20th century, we are currently experiencing a colossal technology race with the rapid advancements in AI. In this information age, it's vital to get children interested in learning about AI and technology – both for their own learning intentions and to help the advancement of AI. However, it's unlikely that many children will be inspired to continue their learning into adulthood, such as teaching themselves additional coding languages, without exciting them about AI technology as early as possible. Therefore, I think the real challenge is for people that facilitate learning with kids to make learning AI fun and exciting. How can we possibly achieve that? Well, why not learn AI through exciting projects? Learn AI through interactive activities – and essentially make learning about AI a mission, and an adventure!

The Importance of Early Engagement with Technology

Children are naturally curious and seek to understand the world around them. So, there is a clear path to harnessing their innate inclinations for learning about the world and applying this when it comes to technology – particularly AI – to give them skills and knowledge that will be useful in the future. First, early engagement with technology is important because young people are more capable than their teachers in the learning process. Second, when young people learn early in life, they can develop an inventive spirit and creative mindset that will help them solve future problems.

1. Futureproofing: As AI enters the mainstream, it's important for us to understand how it works. By getting children into AI from an early age, we can ensure that they can build a solid grounding of knowledge that will be necessary the technology continues to ev

2. Problem-solving: Many AI projects involve building things, which can be fun, but the real reward is in the thinking needed to solve a problem and create – say – an algorithm that bolsters training data for image recognition, or a bot to offer conversational chess tips. Kids get a valuable lesson in taking aims and aspirations and finding solutions, skills that will serve them well in many parts of life.

3. Inspiring Creativity and Innovation: AI can accelerate children's creativity, unleashing their visions and ideas acting as a tool for creative expression.

And they do it in new and exciting ways. Whether designing a game, making digital art or building a robot, AI projects expand a child's thinking about what's possible.

4. Nurturing The Lifelong Habit of Learning: Learning is more fun when it is a pleasant adventure. Transforming AI education into an adventure will inspire kids to explore new things, ask questions, and engage in new learning.

Fun AI Projects to Get Kids Started

Start with fun, low-risk projects to get kids hooked. Here are four ways to entice your child to take the steps that open the door to AI and technology as an artistic, game-like quest, or a fun diversion (or all the above). 1. Introduce voice assistants to create a fun, interactive experience. Begin by speaking to your own voice assistant (such as Siri, Alexa or Google Home) and demonstrate how we can have a conversation with it. Then ask your child to instruct an object to perform a task based on their voice command. This could be as simple as saying: 'Search for pictures of pandas,' or 'Read me a story.' By doing so, you are creating a fun gaming experience. 2. Experiment with artificial intelligence using sustainability-related searches. With the abundance of ecological data available online, you can collect and compare plastics consumption and global temperature charts.

1. Choose-Your-Own Adventure with a Chatbot: A simple chatbot, built in Scratch or using Blockly-style coding, can be a great intro to AI: teach children how to create a chat friend that can answer questions, or have a rudimentary conversation. The project can cover the basics of natural language processing, as well as how to put AI to work in everyday use.

2. Design An AI-Enhanced Game: Game design is a great introduction to AI concepts and, using game design engines such as Unity or Roblox, kids can learn how to create games that introduce AI, from a toy opponent to an adaptive difficulty setting, or even an AI driver in a game. Kids get to engage with a topic of interest, which makes the learning much more fun and engaging for them as well as rewarding.

3. Make Art With AI: Deep Dream: Google's Deep Dream image-processing software is an incredible tool that uses neural networks to turn photos into self-fulfilling prophecies of alternate futures, of dreams gone awry — and of digital deliriousness. Kids 10 and up can use DeepDream to create artwork with AI technologies and learn about neural networks and image processing along the way. This project is all creativity — with a built-in tech-twist.

4. Make and Program a robot: Robotics involves hands-on learning about AI and engineering, as well as giving children immediately rewarding and physically engaging experience. At-home robotics platforms such as LEGO Mindstorms, VEX Robotics, or and Dot let kids build a robot, giving them a concrete object to engage with, then program it to walk, talk, and do the kids' bidding. Kids get to experiment with sensors, algorithms and machine learning.

5. Let's Make Music with AI The technology behind OpenAI's MuseNet – for composing music – might also be a great way to get kids who enjoy music to start experimenting with AI. MuseNet uses machine learning-based systems and vast quantities of data to identify patterns and styles of human-created music, and then uses them to make its own 'original' creations. Kids can give it their own, human, instructions – to generate music with a particular style or tone – and then experiment with the AI's creations. A project that allows kids to interact with technology that combines humans and computers in a creative way.

6. Build a Personal Assistant with AI: Kids love playing with digital assistants such as Siri or Amazon Alexa, and they can now build their own basic version using open-source programmes such as Python and TensorFlow. The project introduces kids to topics such as voice recognition, natural language activation, natural language processing and machine learning so they can understand how these technologies are implemented.

Making AI Learning Accessible

Even though these projects are intended as 'fun' activities for meaningless entertainment, we need to make AI learning accessible to all kids, not only those who have the means to stretch their intellectual curiosity and creativity far outside the box of mandatory computation or discrete mathematics courses beyond university. Some tips for accessible AI education:

1. Make These Things Accessible for Free (or Nearly Free): Fortunately, many of the tools and platforms discussed above are free or low-cost, which means that they can be used by kids of all socioeconomic backgrounds. Insist, when possible, on open-source software and online resources so that everyone has a shot at AI.

2. Opening the digital frontier: Many kids don't have the devices or internet access they need to explore at home. Schools, libraries and community centres can step in by hosting computer labs, coding clubs and community workshops where they can work on AI projects too.

3. Provide Support and Mentorship: Some kids may be unsure of where to start with AI projects. Teachers, parents, and mentors can offer suggestions, answer questions, and provide encouragement to kids tinkering with AI. Tutorials, videos, and other hands-on demonstrations can also make the learning process less intimidating.

4. Make it social: Collaborating on an AI project with peers can make it more fun and less intimidating. Encourage kids to work together on an AI project, either in class, at coding clubs or online. This allows them to share ideas with each other, learn from each other and develop team-working skills.

Conclusion: Turning Learning into an Adventure

As a result, learning about AI doesn't have to seem laborious. On the contrary, kids can find it endlessly fun, creative, and compelling to try out new projects. If fun, interesting, and exploratory activities related to AI become part of how kids spend their free time, then we can turn learning into play, and get kids interested in tech at a very young age.

Consequently, we hold ourselves to a standard of deliberately building a learning space that invites children – our students, our kids, our mentees – to feel excited and motivated by AI, and to want to learn about it. We must intentionally prepare children for these scenarios by offering the resources they need, putting support in the places they access information, and encouraging collaboration with peers and mentors in various communities. In this way, we can foster the next generation of technologists – the ones who'll take the innovations of today and build much more incredible things tomorrow.

Learning AI, too, could be a liberating adventure of making, fixing and inventing – a voyage of AI discovery in which everyone is an equal, and in which learning AI is as playful as it is rewarding, inspiring a lifelong love of technology. Making it fun and accessible will help to achieve that goal.

These articles are still very much about how to make learning about AI interesting, increasingly accessible and beneficial to the next generation of learners. Each article provides practical pointers and actionable project ideas to help teachers, parents and mentors motivate and enable the next generation to acquire important AI skills and develop a love of learning.

CHAPTER 13

The power of AI: how to inspire the next generation of tech leaders

Artificial intelligence (AI) is one of the most powerful and transformative technologies of our time and one of the largest generators of newdocuments and ideas. AI is shaping industries and changing the way we do business. We have never been closer to the ai and robot revolutions envisioned by Isaac Asimov. Artificial intelligence technologies are ambitious, creative and exciting, and will create new opportunities for billions of people who live on the honey pawn. If we are serious about inspiring future technology innovators, entrepreneurs, and leaders, we should all beinformedabout AI. In this article, wedescribe how we caninspire young people to understand, work with and become leaders of this crucial technology of the 21st century.

The Importance of AI Leadership

The pace of progress is such that we will need more and more people trained in the field who will be the leaders of AI and foster innovation. The World Economic Forum estimates that the next generation of AI and related technologies will require the creation of millions of new jobs with many requiring leadership and creative skills.

Becoming an AI leader means more than training to be a development engineer. Students need a broad understanding of the AI ecosystem and its transformative impact on social debates, increasing technical and critical literacy, hands-on familiarity with problem-solving methods, the creativity and determination to set new directions for innovation, and the passion to deliver AI for societal benefit. Lifting young people to be AI leaders means mobilising today's young people who are entering the workforce so that society will have talent ready for whatever AI-related utterance newscasters might imagine tomorrow.

Strategies for Inspiring the Next Generation of AI Leaders

The way to encourage a new generation of tech leaders is not by making things boring and uniform, so that everyone knows what to expect and must mould themselves to fit – but by making them interesting and diverse, awakening curiosity, creativity and entrepreneurial spirit. Some suggestions:

1. Frame the stakes for society: Motivating students to become AI leaders often requires demonstrating to them that AI already makes a difference in their world. Describe real-world examples of the responsible and helpful use of AI to address important social problems (eg, better healthcare, fighting climate change and improving education), and to achieve important social goals.

2. Foster critical thinking and ethical reflection: Leadership in AI demands engaging with ethical issues raised by AI technologies. Challenge students to ask questions such as: How can we ensure that AI is used for good? What are the harms that AI could pose, and how can we mitigate them? Through grappling with these questions, students can learn to think critically about the broader societal implications of AI, as well as build the competencies necessary to lead in this field.

3. Use AI for Entrepreneurialism: many of the most successful tech leaders today (Ray Kurzweil is a good example) were also entrepreneurs who created new products or services using AI. Start teaching students to think like entrepreneurs by encouraging them to identify problems that AI could solve and think through how they could create innovative solutions. Whether you're talking about starting a tech company, designing a new app, or creating a social enterprise, entrepreneurial thinking can help students become AI innovators.

4. Cultivate Leadership: Leadership is a capability developed through experience, so provide AI-focused leadership opportunities. Allow for students to lead a coding club, a hackathon, or to train younger students learning AI confidence building, teamwork, and imparts valuable skills for a career.

5. Connect Students with Role Models and Mentors: Role models and mentors are an important ingredient in developing future leadership among the next generation. Invite AI leaders to speak to students as guest speakers, invite them online to virtual meetups, or give examples of best practice through case studies of leadership within the AI 'community of practice'. And connect students with mentors so that they can receive advice and assistance as they wrestle with learning the art and practice of AI leadership and journey towards leadership themselves. Connecting students with role models and mentors can help them envision themselves as future AI leaders.

The Role of Educators and Parents

It's the teachers and parents who can help to inspire and minister to the next leaders of AI. You can help young people to follow in the footsteps of the big names in AI and become tech leaders – start with these four steps.

1. Growth Mindset: Effective AI leadership requires a growth mindset, meaning the belief that abilities and intelligence can be cultivated through determination and education. Find ways to challenge your students, encourage them to take risks and learn from failure, the inevitable setbacks all students run into, so that they can develop the attitude of resilience necessary to be a leader in the field of AI.

2. Give Students Resources and Learning Opportunities to Explore AI and Leadership: Many students do not have the time or resources to learn about AI or leadership, but we must make sure that they have the resources, tools and learning opportunities to explore how to use AI and apply leadership concepts. Resources for learning how to use AI and coding platforms are readily available and already widely used. Additionally, many universities offer AI courses, but we must also look at introducing leadership training workshops and networking events into high schools and universities.

3. Promote Collaboration and Teamwork: Good leadership often involves collaboration with others to accomplish a goal. Foster collaboration among students on AI projects, whether in the classroom, coding clubs, extracurricular activities or other school-based activities. Collaboration can improve learning, and it aids in developing the working-with-others and verbal communication skills required for leadership.

4. Celebrate Milestones and Successes: Celebrate the students who are 'taking off' in AI and leadership: What milestones and successes have students achieved or accomplished as they learn and grow in their AI and leadership abilities? For example, they might have completed an important and difficult project, won a competition, taken on a leadership role or responsibility, etc. What can you do to honour their milestones and successes or celebrate their progress? You can also take the opportunity to encourage students to consider who else could benefit from their abilities. When you celebrate students' milestones and successes, you can help jump-start their confidence and motivation to keep going and improving as AI and leadership learners.

Conclusion: Empowering the Leaders of Tomorrow

As the new era of AI unfolds, today's youth might someday lead us through it. By inspiring and equipping the next generation of tech leaders, we can usher in the era of AI with a set of heads that are filled, not just with visions of a brighter future, but also with the determination to get there.

This is the role of teachers, parents and others who mentor students in school: to offer the enablement, resources and direction to nurture their leadership in AI –

by igniting their creative appetite, instilling moral reasoning, and encouraging entrepreneurship, particularly among digital natives. This will help to ensure the development of the tech leaders to take their place at the forefront of where AI is headed.

Its power is awesome and can be harnessed for good by systematically cultivating innovation in AI, to the benefit of all, if we smartly invest in the leaders of tomorrow.

DR. SELVA SUGUNENDRAN

CHAPTER 14

Demystifying AI: A Beginner's Guide for Young Enthusiasts

Artificial intelligence (AI) is among the most exciting, dynamic areas in technology. But for young learners, AI can appear daunting or esoteric. How can AI be opened and brought to life in ways that feel intriguing, rather than intimidating, for young people? A first step is demystification – breaking AI down into simple components that make sense to youngsters. This article is a beginner's guide to AI, designed to give young learners a taste of the basics of AI, and inspire them to dive deeper into this world.

What is AI?

Fundamentally, artificial intelligence – or AI, for short – is the science and engineering of making machines, especially software, that can think like human beings. Such machines are then able to perform tasks that we too would struggle to do, like comprehending human language or identifying images, often reaching decisions or learning through experience. The way such tasks work is that AI 'systems' use algorithms – simple instructions about how to do something or perform a task – to process data and come to a decision.

There are different types of AI, ranging from narrow AI, which is designed to perform a specific task (like recognizing faces in photos), to general AI, which has the potential to perform any intellectual task that a human can do. While general AI is still a long way off, narrow AI is already being used in many areas of our daily lives.

How Does AI Work?

AI systems rely on a few key components to function:

1. Data: For AI systems to learn and make decisions, they must have data to work on. This could be data from images, text, sensor readings or any other source, and more data can help AI systems improve their outputs over time.

2. Algorithms: An algorithm is an instruction set that tells the AI system how to process the data and make decisions. There are two kinds of algorithms used in AI: those where the system learns from data to help improve itself (ie, machine learning algorithms) and traditional algorithms.

3. Training: To accomplish tasks, an AI system must be trained. Training involves feeding a system data so that it can bootstrap its learning from pattern recognition. For instance, in machine learning, a new AI system can be trained on 10,000 high-quality images from an online catalog, each one labelled by humans as either a cat image or a dog image.

4. Inference: After it has been trained, the AI system can draw on its knowledge and experience to make new decisions or predictions. This process is called inference. For example, after being trained on images of cats and dogs, it can decide whether a new image contains a cat or a dog.

Fun Ways to Explore AI

Now that we've introduced the basics, here are some easy and fun ways for youngsters to get started in AI:

1. Dabble with AI Tools and Apps: There are so many free tools and apps that novices can use to experiment with AI in ways that don't require any coding. For example, Google has an open-source tool called Teachable Machine that lets people create what's called a 'machine learning model' – basically, the algorithm that tells an AI how to do a job – by providing the AI with examples of what it is supposed to discern. The tool enables you to train the machine to classify things into one of two outputs ('animal' or 'not an animal', or 'yes' or 'no', for example). A similar app called AI Dungeon enables users to create and play text-based adventure games powered by AI.

2. Make a Simple Chatbot: More suited for younger learners is a natural language processing exercise in which students using a block-based programming interface such as Scratch or Dialogflow can create the logic of a chatbot to answer questions or carry out basic conversations.

3. Finally, build a robot, and get it to do stuff. Robotics offers one of the most enjoyable ways of experiencing what AI and engineering are like in practice. You buy a LEGO Mindstorms kit, or a VEX Robotics kit, and you get your hands on a robot that you program to perform various tasks…, or to take commands… – anything that helps it move onwards or gets in its way. It's a hands-on, playful way to understand AI.

4. Experiment with AI Art and Music Generators: For would-be creatives, AI offers tools for creating both art and music. DeepArt allows users to generate AI-powered artwork, while Magenta is a platform that lets you create your own music via machine learning. These tools demonstrate the creative possibilities of the present-day AI and, most importantly, it's fun to play around with them.

5. Take Online AI Classes: There are lots of beginner classes you can take online to help you learn in a more structured way. Coursera, Khan Academy and edX offer classes about AI and machine learning. They also have classes for how to code, which is another skill people sometimes need to enter the field. Many of these online classes offer video lessons, quizzes and projects that can make learning fun and accessible to anyone.

Overcoming Common Challenges

After all, learning AI, like any new skill can take some work. Here are some strategies on how to counter the most common barriers to AI and keep going.

1. Start small: Know that there's no need to bother with learning everything all at once – instead, break down your aspirations into small, manageable chunks of nudgeable territory that match your current skillset, and build confidence from there.

2. Ask for a Channel: If you cannot find an AI channel, you can ask for help here on the MAKE Forum, on Adafruit's forums, or on other online communities or coding clubs.

3. Practice Often: As with all skills, AI performance is intensified through practice. Block out time each week to do a little bit of work on projects, experiment with tools, and play with ideas.

4. Keep Learning: The field of AI is evolving at a fast pace. There is lots to explore and many people working on AI who can generate questions for which you want to find answers. Stay curious, learn continuously and ask questions. The knowledge can also be fun.

Conclusion: The Beginning of an AI Adventure

AI is full of wonder, ripe for exploring and discovering. Breaking artificial intelligence down into basic building blocks makes it approachable and palatable as an area for young enthusiasts to delve into at the earliest stages of their learning journey. This article was first published on Aeon.

That doesn't mean it's hard: the most important thing about AI is to have fun, to enjoy opening the door to learning. Programming a chatbot, teaching your robot to turn your thermostat down when you're away, creating an

AI-powered character for a story, all of these are learning opportunities to be enjoyed.

This beginner's guide to AI is just that: a beginning. In the potent and growing field of AI, the sky is the limit, and your imagination is the only barrier.

CHAPTER 15

From Curiosity to Career: The Benefits of Learning AI Early

We are living today in an era of technology and artificial intelligence (AI) is perhaps the most exciting and impactful field in the world. AI is not just a subject that those working on it are researching, it is a skill that is becoming the most important develop among all professionals in all sectors, and an early learning of AI among young generations can be one of the main paths for discovering a broad career opportunity and a strong base to develop further in life. Through this article, the benefits of learning AI from a young age will be discussed along with the path that can cope with curiosity until discover the gate for a perfect career.

The Growing Importance of AI Skills

AI is transforming society and remaking the world of work in health care, finance and insurance, entertainment, research, education, and beyond. A critical shortage of AI supporters is projected to develop as demand for AI-related skills quickens. Every day, the value of AI is changing the way we live, work and educate. McKinsey has estimated that AI drives up to $13 trillion in worldwide economic value creation by 2030, with much of this based on the contributions of the next generation of AI practitioners.

For young people, learning AI early offers several key advantages:

1. Get a Jump on an In-Demand Field: If you start studying AI early on, you'll get a leg up on a highly desirable field of study. As AI finds its way into nearly every industry and profession, hiring managers are looking for candidates who not only know what AI is about, but can also figure out how to make it work. Getting a jump on AIdata helps students get a jump on potential future careers.

2. Better Ability to Think Out of the Box: Students must possess superior critical-thinking and analytical skills to 'think like a computer' so that they can create AI-based programming: Learn how to analyse, evaluate and reason logically.

3. Better Problem-Solving Abilities: AI promotes excellent problem-solving skills: Learn the problem-solving skills necessary to develop machines that can learn, analyse, and problem-solve: Much like in the fields of mathematics and engineering, these problem-solving skills are valuable in any career that includes decisions about people and processes that involve analysing data and a wide variety of information.

3. Opportunities for Innovation and Creativity: AI is the digital equivalent to a toolbox. It provides young people with a vast array of tools which they can use to create new technologies, solve real world problems and push boundaries of what's possible. Through learning AI, students can discover new aspects of their creativity and develop groundbreaking technologies that can change the world.

4. Career Readiness: The job market of the future will be dominated by AI and related technologies. Students who learn AI early can prepare themselves for jobs of all stripes, from software development and data science to healthcare and robotics. Whether they choose to specialise in AI directly or learn another domain, studying AI from a young age can give them the edge they need to succeed.

How to Get Started with AI

While it can be scary to start with AI if you don't have any friends who know about it, there are many resources that make learning AI a fun and accessible experience for teenagers. Here's a bit of advice for students who wish to embark on their AI journey:

1. Start with Coding: AI is underpinned by code, so this is the first place to take a student who wants to engage with AI. There are introductory coding skills available for all levels and ages. Visual sites such as Scratch, Python and Code.org are enormously engaging and come with fascinating interactive lessons and short-term projects. As skills build, more complex coding languages used in AI can be mastered.

2. Try Out Online Courses in AI: There are many online courses designed for beginners that provide a structured way to learn AI. Websites like Coursera, Khan Academy and edX.org provide courses for individuals interested in learning about the basics of AI and machine learning (and general data science). Courses on these sites typically include quizzes, projects and interactive lessons, which make it fun and easy to learn.

3. Play with AI Tools and Apps: A panoply of free tools and apps (like, for example, Google's Teachable Machine, which requires no coding skills and allows for 'training' simple machine learning models by providing examples of what one wants the AI to learn; or AI Dungeon, a service by which one can both create and play simple text adventure games based on AI models) assist beginners in experimenting with AI. These tools provide a fun and accessible pathway to familiarise future citizens with AI.

4. Join AI Competitions and Challenges: Participating in AI competitions and challenges opens the door for students to apply their skills to real-world situations and put them through the real test. For instance, the AI4ALL Challenge, competitions run by Kaggle, as well as various types of hackathons can help students learn by doing to build and test their AI projects, work in teams with other students, and get valuable experience as they work on AI-related problems. Competitions are also exceptional settings for networking opportunities, mentorship, and authoritative insights from industry experts.

The Long-Term Benefits of Learning AI Early

There are many long-term benefits to learning AI as young as possible that have little to do with school achievement and career success:

1. Lifelong Learning and Adaptation – AI is a rapidly evolving field and learning AI early instills a mindset of lifelong learning and adaptation. The early learner will be the one who continues to ask questions, frequently seek new learning and keep with what is new with AI besting those who start late to AI learning. Adaptability is key in a changing technology world.

2. Confidence and Empowerment: Once students start learning AI and start seeing the effect of their AI work, they will become bolder in believing their own sense of capability and feel empowered to do something and to help the world. As dark filed workers feel confident about their capability and empowered to work on big value creators, they will show more ambition, and become potential prospective leaders of the future.

3. Ethical Consciousness and Responsibility: Learning AI will likely mean living in an AI world. One that will undoubtedly bring impactful changes to society, some positive, others more negative. Early AI learning would help students enhance their awareness of human responsibility in AI development and adoption. It would also make them more adept at questioning the impact of AI on society, and better equipped to use AI in an ethical manner in future careers.

Conclusion: From Curiosity to Career:

AI is a limitless field of opportunity: learning AI early can transform a young person's curiosity and enthusiasm into a fulfilling, valuable career. Starting early means that young people can become AI professionals who can create and lead initiatives in a world where everything is infused with AI.

The goal for all of us – teachers, parents and mentors – is to respect students' curiosity, offer learning opportunities, point to applications that benefit humankind, and encourage them to explore what it will be like to build that road into the future.

The first step on the path from curiosity to career can be taken today. And, with the right support along the way, today's students might be the AI leaders, inventors and change agents of tomorrow.

CHAPTER 16

Engaging the Digital Natives: Innovative Ways to Teach AI

Today's kids have grown up as so-called 'digital natives', accustomed to smartphones, social media and online gaming. We also know they are inquisitive and engaged. It is important that we find innovative ways to teach AI to digital natives. This article describes a series of innovative approaches to engaging kids with AI education and making it fun, interesting, and accessible.

Understanding Digital Natives

Born in the age of the World Wide Web, digital natives (to borrow a term coined by Marc Prensky in 2001) have been raised and have established their skills in establishing and use of technology. In contrast with an earlier generation of digital immigrants, digital natives grow up in a digital world and have become accustomed to a digital way of life. One of the most critical elements of digital natives is the capacity of early adoption of digital technology and embed it as an integral part of their lifestyle.

But while digital natives might be comfortable using technology, they might not necessarily understand how it works or how to build it themselves. That's why it's important to introduce them to the principles of AI in their education. This will help them move from being passive consumers of technology to creators and innovators.

Innovative Approaches to Teaching AI

To maximise our ability to reach digital natives with the message of the potential of AI, we need new pedagogies for 21st-century students who are masters of digital media. Here are some:

1. Convert material to audio form and/or use subtitles to make it available for those who prefer to learn in this way.

2. Create stories with a human element (e.g., people in need of help or political challenges).

3. Focus on the immediate or short-term needs of human beings and political systems.

1. Gamification and Game-Based Learning: Gamification, or the use of game elements to make non-game tasks fun, can be a useful tool to make learning AI as engaging as a game. For example, flipping classroom activities into game-like activities such as earning points, levels and challenges can help students learn and explore AI concepts with gamification. Game-based learning delivers gamification in the form of a game console with challenging questions and fun animations. Through gamified learning, AI concepts can be fun, rewarding and competitive. For instance, Lightbot improves algorithmic thinking by concluding each step with the solution animated on the screen. Similarly, CodeCombat is an excellent platform that simplifies computer science for learners while teaching them about computer science algorithms.

2. Project-Based Learning: Project-based learning is simply providing digital natives an opportunity to work on real-world projects that are meaningful to them and interesting to pursue. In an AI context, examples might be the creation of a chatbot, machine learning model or AI-powered app, among others. Project-based learning encourages learners to learn by doing, collaborate with peers, apply knowledge in meaningful ways, and give them some autonomy over what they are learning (in line with research showing the power of self-regulated learning). It also encourages creativity and innovation by allowing mentored learners to utilise AI as an authentic method for exploring subjects in ways that they find personally interesting.

3. Problem-solving: A core motivation for digital natives is making an impact on the world. Using AI in the context of solving real-world problems is a great way to get students excited. For example, students can use AI to explore environmental data, create tools for improving health care, or work on curricular materials for underserved communities. Demonstrating the power of AI to solve large-scale problems can encourage students to learn more about AI and see the potential of AI for good.

4. Interactive and Hands-On Learning: Many digital natives will find learning about AI more engaging and enjoyable if they can get started on interacting with the technology in a hands-on way, experimenting with tools themselves. Initiatives such as the Google-supported Teachable Machine service enable students to create very basic machine learning models of their own identities, for instance. While more advanced robotics and AI kits, such as LEGO Mindstorms or VEX Robotics, can enable students to build and program robots. Working with tangible materials that can produce real-world outputs allows students to experience AI from the inside so to speak – it might even make it feel like just another tool.

5. Atmosphere and Invention: AI is not only about coding and algorithms – it is also an enabler of invention. Linking AI with invention-based activities such as design, arts, music and storytelling makes it more accessible and makes the subject more interesting for digital natives. For instance, students can create digital artwork with AI tools such as DeepArt or they can create AI-composed musical pieces using tools such as OpenAI's MuseNet. Taking AI out of the laboratory (metaphorically) and linking it to creative practices shows students that AI is not only a technical subject but also a tool with which they can invent, innovate, and express themselves.

Supporting Digital Natives in AI Learning

Just because a digital native is comfortable interacting through technology doesn't mean they don't benefit from support and guidance as they begin their AI experiences. Here are ways to facilitate the process:

1. Give Students Access: Give students access to the resources and online environments where students can play with AI or use AI to create things. Some examples of these are online AI courses, programming environments that can be accessed through a browser, mobile apps that expose students to AI, and robotics kits that students can put together into intelligent, programmable robots. The good news is that most of these resources and environments are free or very low-cost, which allows teachers to use them for widespread use in most educational environments.

2. Encourage Collaboration: Many digital natives are social learners, so rather than going it alone, encourage them to collaborate when undertaking AI projects, such as in the classroom, in coding clubs or online. Collaborative project-based learning enables students to exchange ideas and problem-solve together and learn from each other.

3. Cultivate a Growth Mindset: AI can be difficult to learn, and a growth mindset – the view that one's basic abilities can be developed through dedication and effort – is important to share and reinforce with students. Learning AI can be hard, and it might take some time to get the hang of it. Mistakes are inevitable, and part of the process. Progress takes persistence and effort. Celebrate students' efforts and their successes in learning, creating and jamming. Offer positive feedback when students persevere despite difficulties.

4. Apply it to Their Lives: Make AI applicable to their lives (the things they already use or might want to use soon). For example, if the student is into games, show him/her how to create a game using a high-school friendly game development environment (for example, https://docs.unity3d.com/Manual/GettingStartedInUnity.

html). If the student is into Facebook and other social media, describe AI as applied to recommendation agents.

Conclusion: Engaging the Digital Natives in AI

Digital natives are the future of technology and part of a long-term, generational learning engagement. So, it's crucial to teach them about AI now, not later, since they need to not only learn to use AI but also shape its future design. Gamification, project-based learning and hands-on experience can be successful approaches in engaging young learners in AI education.

Our role as educators, parents and mentors is to equip digital natives with the tools, access and encouragement they need to engage with AI – to reach a point where it can enhance their passions and allow them to thrive in the digital world. If we can make AI education engaging, personally relevant and accessible, we can give the next generation the tools to develop into bold, new age tech innovators and leaders.

Given more support, digital natives can become the inventors, engineers and translators of the world of AI – and the humanising forces changing technology for the better.

CHAPTER 17

AI Literacy: Preparing Young Minds for the Jobs of Tomorrow

There is one fact about life in the first part of the 21st century that is becoming more and more certain: artificial intelligence (AI) is here to stay. From the friendly chatbots you talk to when calling a company's customer service line, to intelligent cars taking us from one place to another, AI is infiltrating how we work, our jobs, our machines, and our modes of travel and life. With the unprecedented speed and reach of AI tools nowadays, knowing about AI is not an advantage anymore: it's a must. For young people, as they prepare for jobs of the future, being AI literate is more important than ever. This article will explain why AI literacy is so important and how to get it.

What is AI Literacy?

AI literacy is the ability to understand, use and critically assess the technology of artificial intelligence and its future development. This includes the technical knowledge and data manipulative skills, but is broader: it involves the societal impact, the social costs and benefits of AI, its ethical use (or misuse) and potential human risks.

But by 'AI literacy' I mean something more than literacy in the sense of how to program a computer. I mean that you understand how AI works; you understand the ways in which it's being used now by different industries and organisations; you understand how it can be applied to new problems; and you understand the benefits it can bring. I think that – over time – AI literacy will come to be seen as just as important to people's lives, jobs and prospects as literacy and numeracy are currently.

Why AI Literacy Matters

Maybe the most important place to look for what tomorrow's jobs will look like is in AI and related technologies. The future of employment will be largely shaped by AI. The World Economic Forum just released a report that estimates AI will create 58 million new jobs by 2022 in fields that are new to us, such as data science, machine learning and robotics. Of course, if millions of new jobs are being added to the economy, it stands to reason that a new set of skills will be needed to communicate and collaborate with technologies we can't even imagine yet. It also means we will need people who can actually sell or design them. This is where AI literacy comes in. Here's why we need it.

1. The Jobs of Tomorrow: When much of the modern workplace is powered by AI, a large fraction of this and that sector's emerging jobs is likely to call for foundational literacy. The whole spectrum of blue- and white-collar jobs, from software development and data analysis to healthcare and finance, requires some foundation in AI. Having AI literacy might become one of the 'T-shaped skills' needed for the digital economy.

2. Support informed decision-making: AI technologies automatically make critical decisions in areas such as finance, healthcare and policing. To make informed decisions about piloting or replacing jobs, regulating autonomous weapon use, or seeking medical or financial services, people need to better understand how AI

technologies work, their biases and limitations, and the implications for society. AI literacy enables one to critically assess AI technologies and their effects on society.

3. Increasing Innovation and Creativity: AI can enhance innovation and creativity in the real world. People can use AI to create new products, services and solutions. By increasing students' AI literacy, people can gain knowledge and skills from AI. And rather than replacing a person's ideas, AI literacy can help individuals apply AI to make their ideas into reality, enabling them to become innovative and influential leaders in the digital age.

4. Cultivating Ethical Awareness: Because AI will have the power to profoundly change our society for good and for bad, true AI literacy will encompass the ethical dimensions of AI systems' potential harm and benefits – issues such as privacy, bias, accountability and more, to ensure that AI technologies are utilised in ways that are beneficial and directed towards the best humanitarian outcomes.

How to Foster AI Literacy

Education can only ensure that young people have the AI-based skills of tomorrow if it places this issue at the centre of their motivation: here are some ways of teaching AI literacy to students.

1. Mainstream AI: AI literacy must be part of the mainstream curriculum. Any student, regardless of income and at any level, must have access to AI literacy. A few options might be to incorporate AI content into existing classes such as math, science and computer science. Teachers can bring in AI content, group projects and AI-related activities to explore AI concepts.

2. Experiential Learning: Any curriculum for developing AI literacy should include experiential learning. Ask students to work on real-world AI projects: having students create a chatbot, a machine learning model, or performing some AI analysis with their own raw data allows them to apply their knowledge in tangible and productive ways and gives them the opportunity to see AI in action.

3. Give Them Access: Make available the resources, tools and platforms that students need to engage with AI. These might include coding environments, online courses, AI apps, robotics kits and more. Many of these tools are free or low-cost, making them available to all sorts of young people.

4. Collaborative and Teamwork-Based Learning: Students can develop their AI literacy through collaboration and teamwork. Get them to work together on AI projects, in class, in coding clubs and other extracurricular activities. In such activities, students get to share ideas, learn from each other, support each other, and solve problems together.

5. Encourage Ethical Considerations: Whether we are discussing children, teenagers, young, or even older working adults, one of the foundational aspects of being an AI citizen should be an awareness of the ethical implications of the technologies we create. This includes not only helping them to unpack how AI technologies could be used for 'good' or 'bad'; it also helps students develop an awareness of what personal and societal responsibilities they might have in relation to AI. For example, for younger students, you might want to discuss issues such as bias in AI technologies, while for older teens or working adults you might want to delve into issues of privacy and social impact that are relevant to AI technologies.

The Role of Educators and Parents

Teachers and parents can help students develop AI literacy in the following ways: Support students to develop AI literacy.

1. Build a Culturally Supportive Learning Environment: Facilitate an environment where students feel safe to tinker with AI and make mistakes, and where we collectively celebrate their successes, provide positive reinforcement, and stick with the process in the face of difficulty.

2. Promote a Lifelong Habit of Learning: AI is a rapidly changing field. Encourage students to develop a learning habit for life: stay curious; search out new learning opportunities; stay aware of new developments in AI. A love of learning will keep them innovating long after they leave school.

3. Enable Self-discovery: Let students experience AI by themselves through activities, projects and other learning opportunities that they can engage with autonomously. These could include programming platforms, AI-enabled educational apps, websites with how-to videos, or other open-source AI tools. Inviting learners to venture on their own fosters a sense of ownership and agency over their own learning and sets the stage for a lifelong passion for discovery.

Conclusion: Preparing for the Future

By teaching courses that impart the skills, literacy, knowledge and aptitudes – and most importantly, the mindsets – necessary for understanding, utilising and appreciating AI, we will be preparing youth for the jobs of the future.

The part we can play in educational settings – as teachers, lecturers, parents and mentors – is to provide the scaffolding that enables students to navigate this path towards AI literacy and flourishing. And that comes through developing a love of learning, fostering ethical awareness, and encouraging creativity and innovation, so that the next generation is equipped for the world they are entering.

Fortunately, the future is bright; with a high-quality education and the right kind of support, today's students can become AI innovators and leaders for tomorrow. Deon's choices offer a tantalising scenario and suggest the importance of equipping children and students with a rigorous and inspiring education so they can succeed in a digital economy.

CHAPTER 18

The Joy of Discovery: Encouraging Young Learners to Explore AI

The field of artificial intelligence (AI) is one of the most promising for innovation and experimentation in the field of technology today. For a budding young learner, AI can be a source of joy as they discover new opportunities for learning and expression. But where does a young learner go to feel joy and enthusiasm about AI? The full potential of an AI ecosystem should encourage exploration and discovery. This blog walks the reader through some ways of cultivating joy and curiosity in young learning environments to engage children of today and tomorrow with AI.

The Power of Curiosity and Exploration:

Curiosity paves the way for learning – for the discovery of things that are worth learning. It promotes initiation in learning; it motivates a learner to ask questions, explore new ideas, and seek the answers to these questions. Students' curiosity makes them more likely to learn information that is consistent with their theories or expectations, to initiate learning activities or strategies, to persist after failures in learning, and to engage in higher levels of self-regulated learning.

This is because exploration literally means finding out new things, in new ways. When advising instructors on adopting AI tools in the classroom in my research, I encourage them to build opportunities for students to explore it as an open-ended technology, through project-based work or experimentation with the existing tools. It's one thing to know what generative AI is, but it's a whole different level to experience what it feels like to explore its creative potential and develop workarounds and new techniques using AI. This sense of ownership over the learning process is important. When my students were given agency to engage with N-Grams, they gained a sense of ownership over the process, instead of feeling like their role was only to assimilate the technology.

Strategies for Encouraging Exploration in AI

To cultivate joy and curiosity in the young learner, dig, drill, dive. Here's how:

1. Think beyond textbooks.

2. Make your walls come alive.

3. Spark imagination.

4. Open connections to resources.

5. Ask questions that provoke inquiry.

6. Model a love for learning.

7. Make the student a co-curriculum designer.

8. Treasure unique strengths and insights.

9. Create hands-on opportunities to learn.

10. Personalise student goals.

11. Take charge of your path.

12. Motivate through reward.

13. Approach with a playful demeanour.

14. Make the learning space flow and feel inviting.

1. Foster a Safe Space for Experimentation: Learning AI is hard, and students will need to experiment, make mistakes, and learn from them as part of their process. Encourage them to take a risk, try something new, do something differently – and make sure that they are recognised for the small and big wins, as well as the inevitable mess-ups. Recognise that making mistakes and clearing up the inevitable mayhem is all par for the course and a powerful bid for struggle.

2. Enable Hands-On Learning: Learning by doing encourages exploration and discovery. Let students work on AI projects, whether building a simple chatbot, programming a robot, or creating a machine learning model. Hands-on learning allows students to apply their knowledge in meaningful ways and see the direct outcomes of their work.

3. Make AI Part of General Learning: AI doesn't need to only live in the computer science classes – it can used in many classes and activities. For instance, students can create AI-assisted scatterplots to support and explore data questions in class, or use AI to create artwork in art class, or generate characters and drama in language arts. By bringing AI to the fore in general learning activities, students can begin to see where AI is relevant to their everyday lives.

4. Let Students Explore: Independently: Let students explore AI on their own terms, with resources and activities that enable learning by play and discovery. Include tools such as coding platforms, AI-powered learning apps, web resources and tutorials, and open-source AI tools. Let students experiment and explore at their own pace, and when they do, they will retain a sense of ownership over their learning and foster a lifelong passion for discovery.

5. Highlight the Joy of Discovery

Celebrate the joy and excitement of discovery. Be sure to celebrate the ease of discovery of new things, like solving a problem or learning the controls for a new AI project.

You can make the same things that make scientific research fun and exciting fun and exciting for your learners. Always celebrate the 'Aha!' moments that make learning fun. It is on the excitement of discovery that you can build motivation for learning.

Making AI Accessible and Fun

You want to get the full benefits of introducing young learners to AI? Make the subject accessible and fun. Here are some ideas to learn about AI the fun way with students:

1. **Use Gamification and Game-Based Learning:** AI education can use the concept of gamification to make learning fun and engaging; for example, by providing points, levels and challenges to incentivise learning and exploration of AI concepts. Gamification is a powerful approach in game-based learning platforms used for teaching coding, such as CodeCombat and Lightbot.

2. **Use It as an Apprenticeship to Creativity:** AI isn't just coding and algorithms. It's also a tool for creativity. Students can incorporate AI into creative projects such as developing video games or digital art or composing music

using AI tools such as Google's Magenta. Combining AI with creative expression can help students see the artistic side of technology. And it might even provide a way for the school-averse creative types to latch on to AI, rather than seeing it as the next black plague.

Offer the Opportunity for Many Students to Work

with AI: Tools and Resources: Offer students the opportunity to work with AI in terms of resources, tools and platforms; making coding platforms and AI-powered apps widely available, as well as robotics kits and online courses. Many of these are available for free or inexpensively and can be made widely available.

4. Let's Do It Together! Exploration is always more fun and enjoyable when it's done with friends. Support students in working together by setting up AI projects in the classroom, coding clubs, or online communities. Collaborative learning enables students to share, develop and refine their ideas, solve problems together, and learn from one other's experiences.

The Role of Educators and Parents

Educators and parents – as well as artificial intelligence (AI) researchers and developers – can contribute to this endeavour in several different ways, a few of which are discussed here.

Here are five suggestions on how to support students as they develop an appreciation for their classmates:

1) Talk about student models

2) Notice student anecdotes

3) Let students take the lead

4) Pair students in different ways

5) Reflect on sense of self

1. Motivation and Praise: Encourage students to explore AI and provide praise when students try, improve or accomplish something in AI. Tell students that learning in AI is hard, that they will have lots of obstacles, and that you will be there to guide them through the learning process.

2. Model a Lifelong Commitment to Exploration: Demonstrate that learning is a 'lifelong' endeavour by keeping up with new ideas and technologies yourself. Make visible contributions – such as writing, sharing new digital tools, attending conferences, and publishing research – while repeatedly sharing your personal experiences of discovery from which your students, too, can benefit.

3. Reward Effort and Successes: Reward effort and successes when students are engaged in AI habits. When a student finished challenging project or learned a new concept, or stepped up to lead an activity, that should be celebrated.

Conclusion: Embracing the Joy of AI Discovery

A playful approach to AI education shows children that exploring AI can be fun and potentially useful One way to do this is by creating a playful environment in which it's fun to learn from situations, and where teachers are delighted in their new-found knowledge. Appreciating the playful nature of learning helps children build the persistence needed to pursue difficult challenges.

The best way for us – teachers, parents, guardians and other guides of students or young persons – to get there is to provide them with desire. More accurately, we need to provide the resources to drive such desire – resources, advice and arguments – to help foster in them a 'love of discovery' for the rest of their lives, to help them understand how to reach for the stars. In this case, the stars are made manifest in the sky of our computational future and can be discovered by learning to harness AI. Interesting work as AI gets larger, older and more connected More 'digital for good': this is AI education made fun and relevant, to help spark the interest of the next generation through new modes of expression, to help them build bridges where humans and computers together can solve real problems and address real-world challenges. These, after all, are the technologies, the practices, that will and should dominate the technological landscape of the times that they inherit from us.

A love of discovery lies at the heart of the learning process, and, by celebrating it, we can help children become the best learners that they can be and the most successful students in a future of intelligence augmentation.

CHAPTER 19

Youth and AI: Cultivating Skills for a Tech-Driven World

Artificial intelligence (AI) is no longer a term of the future. From health and finance to entertainment and education, AI is the innovative force driving the revolution of today in every industry. Now, for young people, picking up AI-skills shouldn't be a choice – it's a necessity. The following article proposes how we can empower young people to develop AI skills, to make them fit for the tech-driven future.

The Importance of AI Skills in the Modern World

At this point, most of us around the world are already interacting with it in multiple ways, from the programs we use to the way we work or communicate. Our growing presence in the virtual world, through more and more advanced algorithms, is constantly fuelling the demand for a new type of worker: someone equipped with AI skills. LinkedIn Technology's most recent 'Emerging Jobs Report ' found that two of the fasting growing skill categories are for AI and machine learning.

Here's why cultivating AI skills in youth is so important:

1. Getting Ready for the Future Workplace: The job market of the future will be shaped by AI and related technologies. Having AI skills will allow young people to get a head start in virtually every job field, from coding or data science to robotics and cybersecurity, because these skills are in high demand in every industry.

2. Enabled Creativity and the Development of New Technologies: Young people can use AI as a tool of creativity to learn how to develop new technologies and solutions to real-world problems.

3. Building Problem-Solving/Critical Thinking Capacity: All students will need to be able to think critically if they are to successfully compete the workplace. The AI-focused curriculum demands such skills, as students work on complex projects, analyse data and develop algorithms that ultimately teach them how to think to solve problems and make good decisions.

4. Cultivating Ethical Awareness and Responsibility: AI will change many aspects of society, both for the better and for the worse. AI development can help students better understand the ethical challenges surrounding AI systems, such as privacy, bias, harm and accountability. AI ethics can help ensure that AI technologies cultivate a benevolent approach to the future.

Strategies for Cultivating AI Skills in You

To do this successfully, we have to create an environment that enables and encourages curiosity, creativity and excitement in technology within education. Here are some suggestions of how to do that.

1. Introduce AI principles exposing young to fundamental notions of AI in an enjoyable and playful environment, for instance using entirely AI-powered learning applications, or coding platforms, or even simple AI tools that enable students to play around and explore AI (in the strictest sense) concepts before or as they learn them. The sooner students are exposed to AI, the better.

2. Embed AI in the Curriculum: Since an AI-based education is important to be available to everyone, AI education can be embedded in the standard curriculum. The basic concepts of AI can be incorporated in subjects like mathematics, science and computer science to make students familiar with AI and the next generation computing paradigm. Teachers can also involve various AI-related projects and activities to motivate students in learning and exploring AI in an engaged manner.

3. Promote Tinkering and Experimentation: Hands-on learning is one of the most important learning tools for helping students acquire AI skills. Encourage students to get involved in real-world AI development project activities, such as developing a chatbot, building a machine-learning model, or trying to analyse data through AI tools. This way, students will be able to apply what they learned in practice and feel like they are creating an AI that is making a difference.

4. Promote Collaboration and Teamwork: Collaboration and teamwork are often required for producing AI, so students should be encouraged to work together by offering AI project requirements in a classroom, a coding club or any kind of after-school activity. Collaborative learning allows students to brainstorm, problem-solve and share ideas to learn from each other's perspectives.

5. Give Access to AI Resources: Make sure that students have access to a coding platform that exposes them to fundamental programming theories; online courses to accompany learning; AI-powered apps that provide exposure to machine learning; and robotics kits. There are many options available and quite a few are either free or inexpensive, making access available to students from a wide range of socioeconomic backgrounds.

6. Integrate Ethics of AI: Ethical considerations should be given a significant portion of instruction on AI. Have your students ask questions about the ethical implications of AI technologies and how this technology can be implemented responsibly. Discussions about AI bias, data privacy and ethics, and the social impact of AI can equip your learners with a nuanced and holistic view of AI.

Supporting the Development of AI Skills

Educators, parents and mentors all have a role to play in facilitating young people's AI skills. Here are some of the ways to encourage learning in AI.

1. Help students to study and understand the historical development of AI. Provide a historical background to help students gain a better understanding of the present.

2. Understand students' misconceptions about the future of AI. Better communication and curiosity can help improve the use and development of AI for people's wellbeing.

3. Use classroom case studies based on real problems to help students better memorise theoretical knowledge and related concepts.

4. Encourage students to think about the social and economic consequences of AI, rather than purely technical issues.

5. Designing instructional scaffolds that provide learners with a safe place to experiment with AI and learn from their mistakes. Our findings suggest that for students to feel comfortable using AI, your classroom must be designed to reward such exploration – providing positive reinforcement for learned strategies, and pushing them to keep going when they encounter challenges.

6. Enable Autodidactic Learning: Allow students to explore AI independently. Offer time, tools and topics they can pursue on their own to foster autodidacticism. AI makes the perfect subject to experiment with – there are many code platforms and AI-based learning apps, as well as web tutorials and open-source AI-tools they can tinker with at their leisure. Giving students control over their learning path and encouraging their own explorations will encourage them to gain a sense of agency over their learning process and foster a lifelong love of discovery.

7. Promote a Growth Mindset: Learning AI may be hard in the short term, but it can get easier with practice. By fostering a positive 'can-do' mindset, students can be reassured and reminded that the brain is like a muscle that gets stronger with exercise, and that reflecting on and learning from mistakes can lead to success, not failing. Be sure to praise every form of effort and growth, consider all forms of progress, and celebrate students achieving new milestones and solving difficult problems.

Conclusion: Cultivating Skills for the Future

The world is changing because of AI. The skills needed to understand and navigate it will become more important to your success. Teaching AI skills to today's students prepares them for tomorrow in a tech-driven world and empower them to become the innovators, leaders, and changemakers of tomorrow.

We need to be teachers, parents or any other kind of mentor who help provide the space, tools and know-how to make the most of artificial intelligence: allowing students to find and pursue their own path, cultivating a passion for lifelong learning, instilling ethical sensibilities and encouraging imagination and innovation. It is only by doing so that we can set the younger generation up for much taller skies ahead.

The future, however, looks bright: given the right educators and support systems, the next generation could well be the AI masters, creative innovators and community change agents of tomorrow.

CHAPTER 20

Turning Imagination into Innovation: How AI Can Inspire Young Creators

Imagination forms the foundation for creativity and innovation. It fuels young people's dreams and the motivation to explore the unknown. While vast layers of digital technology link our societies, one innovation has the potential to become a major driving force for imagination and innovation in the future. Artificial intelligence (AI) systems can play an essential role in transforming imagination into innovation – and in doing so, open innovation to young people as a project in a way that previously seemed impossible. In this article, we show how artificial intelligence can spark young people's creativity and empower them to become innovators and creators and discuss how we should support their endeavours.

The Intersection of Imagination and AI

AI is not just a technical tool. It's also a creative medium and, like many forms of technology, a blank canvas. There is an expansive range of creative and playful applications for text-detection software, including using artificial intelligence to generate art and music, design video games, and even tell stories. In doing so, young creators can hone their creative problem-solving skills and embrace the unique imaginations of children.

Here are some ways in which AI and imagination intersect:

1. AI-generated Art and Music: One of the things AI could be used for are original, AI-generated art forms and the music related to them. Young creators could explore new styles and techniques using AI image-processing software such as Google's DeepDream and OpenAI's MuseNet to have a whole new cell in which to create. When used in tandem with a human's imagination, AI has the power to cross-pollinate and transform entire domains into new expressions.

2. AI-Augmented Storytelling: Beyond merely engaging in games, AI can be used to help young users craft interactive narratives and the foundations of games. Systems such as AI Dungeon or StoryStream enable AI-assisted, interactive, two-way storytelling built on user-provided input, the system generates a storyline that is shaped as the narrative progresses. In this way, AI can help young users craft new kinds of interactive and dynamic stories and narratives, engaging an audience who feel more included in the experience of the telling of the story itself.

3. Designing and crafting AI-enabled gaming environments: People around the world have long used video games to express their creativity, and AI can play a part in allowing young people to create games that are richer and more varied than ever before. AI can be applied to creating more dynamic and intelligent non-player characters (NPCs), generating adaptive difficulty levels and creating ever more interesting environments through procedurally generated worlds. Young creators can design AI-enabled gaming environments that enable players to play in ways that have never been possible before.

4. Practical Problems, Real-World Applications: AI is an outstanding tool for problem-solving. And once again, young creators can also harness the power of AI to solve problems and goals that are practical and relevant for today's world and community. AI can be used to explore environmental data, develop healthcare applications, or create instructional resources for classrooms and beyond.

Strategies for Inspiring Young Creators with AI

To train a generation of creators who are comfortable with AI's capabilities, it's essential to develop an environment for learning that's open-ended and quintessentially human. How can we accomplish this? Here are some ideas.

1. Let them get creative with AI: Encourage students to use AI as a creative tool, by engaging with digital manipulation, e.g. developing their own video games, digital art or composing music with AI software. Exciting students to try AI creatively might help them to appreciate the artistic side of technology and see AI as a tool of innovation, not just another technical subject.

2. Encourage Collaboration/Shared Idea Exchange: Collaboration fosters innovation, and students ought to be encouraged to collaborate on AI projects. Whether it's within the classroom walls, at a coding club or through extracurricular activities, students working collaboratively allows for students to share ideas, solve issues and collaborate while developing the teamwork and communication skills needed for creative innovation.

3. Give Them the Resources to Work with AI: Make sure that students have opportunities to get their hands on different AI tools – whether these be coding platforms, AI-powered apps, robotics kits or online courses – and learn from experts and peers. Many of these resources are now free or low-cost and are openly available for most students. This would give students the opportunity to develop and test ideas and use them to create products.

'AI needs imagination' At every step, encourage decisions that require creative thinking, and make it 'AI can help with creativity, but students should be made aware at every step that AI may help them complete a task, but that needs them to make creative about how to complete the work. Emphasise that the AI needs imagination! Here are three examples of student decision-making that are ripe for creativity-boosting explanations: (i) 'Ask questions about the pairings of the lines of text' (ii) 'Ask questions about the pairings of the lines of text'. To complete the problem, students must pair the lines of text and then decide whether the proposed summaries are too concise or too long-winded. (iii) 'AI can help with creativity, but creativity is essential for AI. AI needs imagination.' (iv) Ask students to think about what the data might be revealing about the writer's argument. Encourage them to ask questions about the pairings of the lines of text and what those questions reveal about the writing. At every step, encourage decisions that require creative thinking

(v) Celebrate Creativity and Innovation: Celebrate your students' creative innovations with AI. If they complete a difficult education project, or they hack a new game, or create AI-generated artwork, or somehow are using AI as part of their creative journey, celebrate these milestones. By calling out their creativity, you can help students believe in their power to innovate and be excited about what comes next.

Supporting Young Creators in AI

As educators, parents and mentors, we have the unique opportunity to support these young makers as they use AI as a tool to expand their creative abilities. Here are some helpful ways to support a child's journey.

1. Encouragement and Positive Reinforcement: Encourage students to use AI in creative ways and reward them with positive reinforcement when they reach a goal or achieve a milestone. Guide and support them through the creative process when challenges emerge and encourage them to try and fail before succeeding.

2. Provide a Safe Zone for Experimenting: A learning space that offers a safe zone for experimentation provides the sense of protection that fosters creative thinking. Begin by guaranteeing that students' experimentation is allowed and expected, and that students can make bad choices and practise the art of failing. Applaud the wins but be equally clear that trial-and-error is a hallmark of creativity and that it's perfectly okay not to get everything right.

3. Encourage a Growth Mindset: Learning AI and learning to use creative ideas to build something is hard, and we need to support a growth mindset i.e. the belief that your basic abilities aren't fixed traits (as years of study now tell us) but can be nurtured and developed through dedication and hard work. We need to encourage students that creativity is a process, that persistence and practice will help them to become master AI coders and realise their ideas.

Conclusion: From Imagination to Innovation

Possibilities of imaginative play leading to pathways of invention are amplified by AI's ability to turn imagination into actual innovation. Young creators who are encouraged to envision solutions, such as new ways of playing or feeling or going about their physical, virtual and environmental worlds, can test those ideas in AI and thereby experience reality gained through dream. The Writer's AI learns from its interaction with its developer/user and becomes better at morphing itself into whatever depth of imagination is presented – could it one day learn that forms are interchangeable, about deepening our own evolving structure, about meditating on layers of possibilities? The 'creator machine' is here to stay, we are it, it is us: AI lies somewhere between our dreamtime and wake-time, daydreams and literary imagination, the private creative Imagination (capital 'I') and 'I think', the generative and the received, and holds the potential of transmitting those energies between one another.

Our obligation as teachers, parents and mentors is to give them whatever resource or support we can to understand what their creative journeys might be, and help them to succeed in the world with which they will likely be most closely aligned: the world of machines

What kind of technologies keep coming? Far too often, imagination gets in the way of that process. But if kids are encouraged to create with AI, the technologies that get made next will be those that originate in their imaginations. Our current crop of creative young people is our chance to help shape the future of AI, and we need to empower them to have a significant role in that.

CHAPTER 21

Learning AI Through Play: How to Make Technology Fun for Kids

Artificial intelligence (AI) is a synonym for technical revolution – a sea change that holds promise for humankind's development. However, no matter how necessary AI is for the future, introducing children to such a seemingly incomprehensible subject can be a daunting task. You may have doubts about the central concept of AI/robotics being suitable for kids at the early stages of their development. Or it could be your own lack of understanding that makes you think it is impossible to teach AI at all.

Teaching complex subjects such as AI to kids seems like a mammoth task. However, let me share a few tips and strategies for introducing this fascinating subject to children in a way that by giving children an opportunity to play with AI concepts, we make the prospect of technical revolution and its ever-growing usefulness for people entertaining, fun and comprehensible.

To be fair, I'm not the originator of the concept of learning-through-play. This idea was developed decades ago by experts in child development and education, who view learning-through-play as a universal approach for raising children. Whatever subject or area you're teaching, this technique can be successfully applied. All you need to do is delve into the technical matters less, and provide some playful, qualified support for your child. Rather than focusing on facts, I argue that AI learning-through-play involves the nurturing of a child's emotional and psychological skills.

The Importance of Play in Learning

Play is an essential part of growing up, so learning presented as play is more likely to be engaging. It's more interesting, and children are more motivated, more involved and more ready to take on challenges.

Play-based learning aims to upend that paralysis by teaching the fundamentals of AI through games, interactive activities and hands-on projects that are not only fun but offer the opportunity for children to experiment, problem-solve and create. Play-based education will instil a positive attitude towards technology and cultivate a love of learning.

Strategies for Teaching AI Through Play

To engage students with play-based learning activities and gameplay that demonstrates how AI can be used, add a little fun to your teaching using gadgets and gizmos: - Allow students to engage critically with technology through freeform play.

Allow students to explore layers of interactivity with loose parts.

-Incorporate other toys like aliens, rockets, and dinosaurs, along with books, music, and technology, into activities.

- Encourage students to unplug and start drawing!

1. Gamify Learning: What better way to build an incentive for learning by using elementary principles of gaming, where points, levels, and challenges facilitate learning and playing at the same time? Some apps such as CodeCombat, Lightbot and Tynker are already using gamification within their systems to instruct young users in the fundamentals of coding and AI. Kids are presented with challenges that aid learning, material and rewards are provided as a means of motivation, and they progress to further games as they progress. These gaming apps do not seem like learning platforms at all; rather, learning seems more like 'gameplay' rather than education.

2. Teach kids AI with interactive AI toys and robots: The hands-on, interactive nature of robotics and AI toys is another way to introduce kids to AI. The fields of robotics and AI are expanding rapidly, with new products coming to the market every year. If you're looking for a robot or AI toy for your child, there are a plethora of options available. You probably don't even have to leave your home: Amazon has an entire shelf devoted to AI and robotics toys! And there is no shortage of options when it comes to evaluating the products.

YouTube channels, like Dot smith Toys, host lucrative 'Amazon robotics toy wars', providing hours of video to help sift through the broad range of choices. LEGO Mindstorms, Dash and Dot, Cozmo, and a plethora of other robotics and AI-infused toys are designed for learning about robotics and AI through play.

These toys enable children to build and program their own robots and, in doing so, learn about sensors, algorithms and machine learning in a fun and playful environment. As they play, kids are not even aware that they're learning AI.

3. Generate AI-Powered Projects and Games: Allow your kids to create their own AI-powered games and projects. There are numerous platforms where your kids can make their own games using AI elements and tools, such as Scratch and Roblox, to program video games with AI designing aspects, like intelligent monsters.

By playing makers of their own games, children are given a rich context in which to engage with AI concepts and learning can be arduous and intellectual, or it can be playful – fun can become intertwined with learning itself.

4. Make AI Part of Play: AI doesn't have to stay behind classroom doors. Kids can be introduced to AI through apps that facilitate digital art, music and storytelling, or create Minority Report-like digital arcade-games, using AI tools such as Google's Magenta or DeepArt. Kids can master the basic concepts of machine learning by engaging in everyday, screen-based play. They can easily see how AI becomes part of their life, increasing buy-in and interest.

5. Foster Collaborative Play and Learning: Children can often learn most from Play when they do it with others. Foster kids to work together in collaborative AI projects – whether that's in coders' clubs, at school, or online. Collaborative play can allow kids to devise solutions, discuss ideas, and learn from each other. Doing so can also help kids foster teamwork and communication skills and make the learning experience more social and enjoyable.

Supporting AI Learning Through Play

Educators, parents and mentors can play a vital part in facilitating playful AI learning. Here are some ways to experiment with and scaffold playful AI learning for kids.

1. Make Play-Based AI Available: No child is going to play with AI unless it's readily available to them. Engage kids with play by giving them access to the tools and platforms they need to explore AI, such as learning to code, using AI-powered toys, playing with robotics kits, and taking online courses. Much of this is already free or low-cost and available to a range of students.

2. Show Them and Then Let Them Go: Support your kids' ideas and encourage them to 'play' with AI tools and projects, even when they aren't sure of the final output. Encourage them to experiment and remind them that 'play' is a time for exploration and testing, mistakes and learning. In the pursuit of keeping kids engaged and happy, a simple age-appropriate way to encourage kids to make their own AI tools and projects is to just get out of their way and let them explore AI in individual ways and at their own pace. Giving kids the freedom to explore and learn with AI at their own pace might seem counterintuitive, but it is one important way in which we can help kids feel a sense of ownership over their learning and thus strengthen the bonds that Atkinson describes that lead to a lifelong love of learning.

3. Celebrate Successes and Milestones: Recognise the achievements and milestones of your AI child. Whether it's completing a difficult project, grasping a new AI concept, or making an AI game, recognising milestones reinforces children's confidence and continues to motivate them to keep learning.

4. Make Learning Playful: Incorporate playful elements into the learning experience and create interactive, hands-on learning environments such as a coding corner with AI toys and robotics kits, AI-themed game nights or even coding competitions. With learning that's playful and interactive, kids stand a chance at developing a positive attitude towards technological solutions and the curiosity of learning about those artificial intelligences.

Conclusion: Making AI Learning Fun

AIs are indeed powerful, and the field is very exciting – so it's important that we teach them in ways that both kids and adults find fun and meaningful. Gamification, hands-on toys and creative projects are a great place to start.

By supporting and encouraging students to play with AI, we adults – as educators, parents and mentors – need to provide the resources and opportunities for kids to experiment, learn about, and learn from AI in a fun and meaningful way. Playful AI learning can enable our young tech visionaries to dream up the next big thing and positively impact our future world technology.

When it comes to teaching AI, the process can become a game of exploration and innovation, of discovery and fun. Aid them accordingly, and today's children just might become tomorrow's AI captains of industry.

CONCLUSION

Shaping the Future: The Impact of AI Education on the Next Generation

As we end this journey of AI education for learning youth, it's crystal clear that AI is never gonna stop changing the world. It is not just technology, but a force that has been and will keep changing the world. For the next generation not learning AI means not being able to work more and more for living in the world.

In this book, we've covered a range of key themes for teaching and learning with AI, from playful, motivating learning; creative, transdisciplinary and imaginative learning, and the development of agency. We've looked at introducing AI via play, AI and a growth mindset, and preparing young people for jobs that don't even exist yet. What unites all these discussions is the assumption that every young person can become a maker, an innovator, and a leader in the AI age.

Just as filling cavities or treating broken bones requires a certain skill set, so does engaging with AI. By preparing students with AI skills, we make sure that they are ready for jobs in the technology-driven society around them. We give them what they need to be effective contributors to the common future that is being built by the convening power of AI. We do this by preparing students to learn about the technology around them, use it creatively, employ it ethically, and make a positive contribution – a contributing technology as we say. We equip today's youth to tackle tomorrow's problems, anticipate creative innovations, and contribute to a world that relies on AI.

It is a path that we must travel together, as parents, teachers, mentors and a community. It means committing to give young people the resources, support and inspiration to learn about AI, and to explore what might be possible. It means believing in young learners, encouraging their curiosity, and demonstrating ethical responsibility.

The 21 articles in this book map a path towards those goals, with practical ways to invoke imagination in younger learners, to prepare them to meet the realities ahead, to enrich them intellectually and culturally, and to motivate lifelong journeys of discovery, wonder and ongoing learning. AI education isn't only about technical training: it is about how we instill the love of learning, build curiosity, foster imagination and empower tomorrow's citizens to become true adventurers, imbued with the confidence to engage resources for themselves.

And the future is full of possibilities. Next generation can be creators of tomorrow's world, where AI means "responsible AI", responding to human imagination to create a new and more equitable world. Investing in AI education is investing in a future and in a future generation of young people who will shape that world.

The learning journey of AI has just begun, and the benefits to the children of today and tomorrow will be enormous – to help young people develop their talents, to aim for the stars and yes, every single day, to learn to lead.

You've been with us on this. The future is in our hands. But with young people led and encouraged – and with enough planning, teaching, modelling and support – it can be a rich experience and indeed an exciting journey.

PART II
Selected Books by the Author

These books can be viewed/ bought by following the link below to the Amazon site:

https://selvasmail.com/selvasbooks

Alternatively, should you wish to view the books on your phone or tablet, you could scan the barcode below, which will also take you direct to the Amazon site.

DR. SELVA SUGUNENDRAN

BOOKS ON WELLNESS & HEALTH (7 BOOKS)

BOOK ON ALZHEIMER DEMENTIA (6 BOOKS)

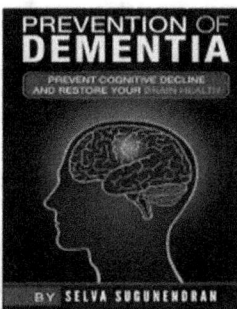
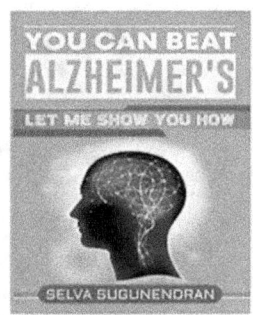

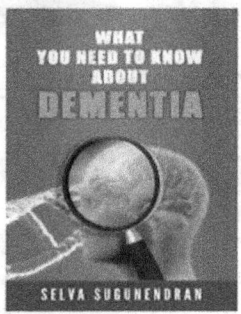

BOOKS ON SUCCESS (5 Books)

AI UNLEASHED: SPARKING INNOVATION AND CURIOSITY IN YOUNG MINDS

BOOKS ON AI ROBOTICS (9 BOOKS)

CHRISTIAN BOOKS (18 BOOKS)

  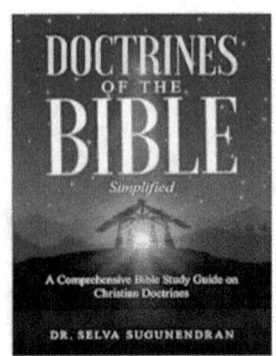

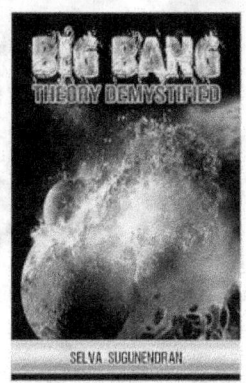

APPENDICES

1. WEBSITE LINKS

http://AIRoboticsForGood.com

http://MyChristianLifestyle.org

http://BlessMeLord.com

http://HealMeLord.today

http://CreationEvolutionAndScience.com

http://AIRoboticsForGood.com

http://DementiaAdvice.care

http://HowToLeadAVibrantLifeWithAlzheimers.com

2. CONTACT LINKS:

The Author EMail: **Selva@AIRoboticsforGood.com**

All Books by Author Available on Amazon:

https://selvasmail.com/selvasbooks

www.ingramcontent.com/pod-product-compliance
Lightning Source LLC
Chambersburg PA
CBHW052314220526
45472CB00001B/115